T0361437

Strategic Listening

Listening is so simple, yet so difficult. Many times, listening is taken for granted. One could therefore say that listening is the forgotten part of communication. Although organizations have more digital and analog communication channels than ever, too little time is spent listening to customers, employees, and other influential groups. It is a shame that listening is not given more attention, as it is linked to many positive values. Examples include better conversations, increased trust and confidence, more outstanding commitment and job satisfaction, lower absenteeism due to illness, higher productivity and quality of work, increased sales, better relationships with customers and employees, and many other positive effects. To the extent that listening takes place, organizations rarely take a holistic approach to it. Strategic listening means a given objective for listening, thoughts about who should listen, when it should happen, and so on. An organization's listening must become a strategic issue to exploit the great potential of increased listening.

This book provides answers to the following:

- Why is listening important?
- What are the barriers to listening?
- How can both individuals and organizations become better at listening?
- How can organizations develop strategic listening skills?
- How does one build a system to improve an organization's strategic listening?

Mats Heide is a professor at the Department of Strategic Communication at Lund University, Sweden.

Anette Svingstedt is a senior lecturer at the Department of Service Studies at Lund University, Sweden.

Strategic Listening

How Managers, Coworkers, and
Organizations Can Become
Better at Listening

Mats Heide and Anette Svingstedt

Routledge
Taylor & Francis Group

A PRODUCTIVITY PRESS BOOK

First published 2024
by Routledge
605 Third Avenue, New York, NY 10158

and by Routledge
4 Park Square, Milton Park, Abingdon, Oxon, OX14 4RN

Routledge is an imprint of the Taylor & Francis Group, an informa business

© 2024 Mats Heide & Anette Svingstedt

ISBN: 978-1-032-53767-2 (hbk)
ISBN: 978-1-032-53766-5 (pbk)
ISBN: 978-1-003-41348-6 (ebk)

DOI: 10.4324/9781003413486

Typeset in Sabon and Optima
by Apex CoVantage, LLC

Contents

Authors

Mats Heide is a professor of strategic communication at the Department of Strategic Communication, Lund University. Together with his colleagues, Mats introduced the field of strategic communication in Sweden. Almost 20 years ago, he was the first to write about strategic communication in a Swedish book. Since 1995 he has researched social media and organizational learning, change communication, crisis communication, and professional studies on communication practitioners. In 2014–2018 he was the project leader of one of the world's largest research projects on communicative organizations. In this project, Mats became aware of the importance of strategic listening. Mats is the author and co-author of 15 books and many book chapters and articles. He has written several textbooks on strategic communication, organizational communication, and crisis communication. Mats also work as a consultant, lecturing, advising, and networking for both private companies and public organizations.

Website: www.isk.lu.se/mats-heide
LinkedIn: www.linkedin.com/in/matsheide

Anette Svingstedt is a senior lecturer in service studies at Lund University. She has had a 20-year management career in the private sector in industries such as hotel and tourism. Anette has been a manager, partner, and CEO in these businesses. During these years, Anette's interest and commitment to leadership in service businesses were nourished. In 2012 she obtained her PhD in service studies. The thesis aimed to increase the knowledge of how the business logic is embedded in service encounter practices. She studied service encounters in a hotel, an elderly care and in a Swedish court. Since her PhD, she has researched value creation in service, leadership, mobile shopping, slow and sustainable travel and sustainable services.

Anette has written articles and book chapters on these topics. She also work as a consultant, lecturing, advising, and networking for both private companies and public organizations.

Website: www.ses.lu.se/anette-svingstedt
LinkedIn: www.linkedin.com/in/anette-svingstedt-87446b89

Preface

WE ARE TWO individuals who are good at listening, at least in our opinion. During the work with this book, we have reflected on the power of listening in many different situations—both privately and professionally. We had experienced both situations when the listening functioned perfectly and when it was completely absent and led to a lot of criticism and dissatisfaction. Unfortunately, so far, the negative cases are more than the positive ones. There are many occasions when we have ended up in meetings or next to people who took up all the speech space and who were totally absorbed by themselves and their thoughts, and they completely forgot to ask questions and listen to the rest of us. Mutual listening is totally lacking. After a while, when you feel neither seen nor heard but only become a container into which the other person pours their stories, the interest in really listening wanes. This is a shame because we all deserve to be listened to. Humans are interesting; have different experiences, knowledge, ideas, thoughts, and opinions; and deserve to be listened to. And being listened to is an essential factor for all of us to make us feel good:

To be heard and understood is perhaps the most precious gift in life.[1]

This book has arisen due to many long discussions about the importance of listening between Mats Heide, professor of strategic communication, and Anette Svingstedt, senior lecturer in service studies at Lund University. Through our conversations, we have realized that both of our research fields, management and communication, are closely related, and by drawing from different perspectives, we develop new knowledge that can be used to make significant changes in organizations. By listening and learning from different areas of research, we contribute to the development of knowledge. Many organizational changes fail because different departments or professions fight internally over who owns a particular issue. But if one can succeed in changing the way organizations function and develop them to work more cross-border, they will be more efficient and successful. To work across borders and break down silo structures that are common in organizations means that you must listen and learn from each other. That's when successful changes can take place. And there would then be less tension between coworkers in organizations. The former CEO of SAS, Jan Carlzon, notes:

> *I genuinely believe that we would have fewer misunderstandings and fewer conflicts if we could take each other in and listen to what others have to say.*[2]

The book *Strategic Listening* is aimed at everyone in an organization—in both the public and private sector—who is interested in strengthening relationships and trust with various stakeholders and between coworkers and managers. This book is essential for managers, quality managers, HR specialists, communicators, project managers, account managers responsible for innovation and development, and many other organizational functions and roles. The book also aims at students taking organizational, leadership, and communication courses in business administration, sociology, psychology, service management, media and communication studies, and strategic communication.

Falsterbo, Sweden, September 2023
Mats Heide and Anette Svingstedt

Introduction

THE ANCIENT PHILOSOPHER Aristotle argued that all knowledge begins in wonder. Our great wonder of listening and strategic listening is the starting point for this book. We are amazed by the built-in paradox of the inherent human need to listen. But does listening solely entail "opening" the ears and taking in what other people are saying? No, listening can be challenging to practice and master. Most of us have experiences of failed listening, and we know that listening is not easy, no matter how much we want and try to listen to others. Many obstacles make it difficult for us to listen, and precisely this paradox arouses our wonder. The paradox of listening constitutes the most important reason why we have written a book about strategic listening. Our ambition is to spread knowledge about the incredible power of listening, which seems to be a forgotten component in communication. Despite the increased use of digital communication channels that offer many opportunities for dialogue and listening, the focus is still mostly on conveying information to influence the perception of others. Informing and disseminating information is not nearly as effective as involving others and listening to them:

Even in a world of limitless, instantaneous, global connection, the most powerful mode of communication is that of two people listening.[1]

A Book about Strategic Listening

We believe that a more strategic approach to listening is needed in contemporary organizations. Even though there currently is a lot of listening going on, a holistic approach to listening is still missing. Different kinds of listening take place locally in the organization, here and there, for example, managers who are good at listening and affirming their coworkers or coworkers who listen to customers or users. Listening is thus scattered. But the question is whether there are any objectives for listening, ideas of who should listen, when it should happen, and so on.

The first step in developing an organization's listening is for the management team and other managers in the organization to consider listening as a strategic issue. By the term managers, we mean all those with various functions as formally appointed managers. This includes functions such as project managers, innovation managers, sports managers, and team leaders or other designations of the managerial role. There is a need for managers at all levels to start talking about strategic listening in the organization. By strategic listening, we mean that listening is conscious, reflective, goal-oriented, and systematized in the organization. What follows is our definition of strategic listening.

Definition of Strategic Listening

STRATEGIC LISTENING is the relationship-oriented, goal-oriented, and systematized listening of organizations that creates the conditions for successful operations.

Strategic listening requires a management that focuses on listening when organizing, leading, and controlling the business.

Strategic listening makes demands on organization, management, governance, and training.

Thus, strategic listening increases the ability to manage complex and rapid change inside and outside the organization, as listening can provide important information and knowledge.

Listening needs to be highlighted and made a more explicit issue to be discussed and problematized. This book offers help to problematize organizational listening and to improve both individuals' and organizations' knowledge and ability to listen. The book provides answers to questions such as:

- Why is listening important?
- What barriers to listening might exist?
- How can both individuals and organizations become better listeners?
- How can organizations develop strategic listening skills?

This book is for anyone who wants to understand the importance of listening to individuals and organizations and learn how people and organizations become better listeners. Effective listening is a skill that needs to be practiced, and this book gives you the tools to develop that skill.

Why Is Listening Important?

Successful managers always start by answering *why* when trying to convince their listeners.[2] We will begin this book by answering why listening is vital for individuals and organizations.

In a modern society such as ours, listening is more necessary and complex than ever. This is partly due to the vast amount of information available to us. That makes it challenging to know which people or groups to listen to. Today, there are both demands and expectations for managers in organizations to listen to coworkers, customers, and other stakeholders. They, in turn, expect to have their voices heard. Newer ways of working and organizing activities in teams and matrix structures mean higher demands for collaboration, cooperation, and listening in today's organizations. In times of crisis, such as during the Covid-19 pandemic, listening has been an important factor in building and maintaining internal trust in organizations.[3] In people-to-people communication, listening is a particularly important element in creating and maintaining good relationships, trust, and psychological safety.[4] Research shows that when managers are poor listeners, it can lead to higher turnover, coworker burnout, dissatisfaction, and low engagement.[5] The same research also shows that high-quality and genuine listening can strengthen relationships and lead to better results for individuals and organizations.

In too many organizations, disseminating information is valued more than listening.[6] A clear example of when communication is mainly focused on information dissemination is during significant planned organizational changes. In a study by Lewis, she concluded that managers spend far more time disseminating information about the change to coworkers than listening to their questions and concerns.[7] The focus on disseminating information and not listening during ongoing changes also explains the failure of as many as 70 percent of organizational changes.[8]

Asking managers and coworkers in organizations reveals a big gap between the rhetoric of what should be done and what is done in practice. In a major European survey—the European Communication Monitor (ECM)—conducted since 2007, 93 percent of responding communication professionals consider listening to be the most critical skill that needs to be developed.[9] Hence, listening skills are crucial for organizations to build and maintain trust. In the same survey conducted in 2021, trust was identified as the most important strategic area for organizations.[10] If we look at communication training, almost all focus on informing, speaking, persuading, disseminating, and influencing others. This means that managers, marketers, human resources (HR) strategists, communication professionals, and others trained in communication are not taught how to become better listeners. The strategic value of listening is consequently ignored, and listening is mainly seen as something of little value, although people have since long known the great value of listening. In 1936, Dale Carnegie stressed in his book *How to Win Friends and Influence People* that the primary way to be successful as a business leader, a salesperson, or anyone who wants to build good relationships is to be a good listener.[11]

In many organizations, internal structures and processes are usually created for external listening, while internal listening is more taken for granted, as managers seem to focus on informing coworkers rather than listening to them. Many resources are spent on listening to external stakeholders such as customers, users, and citizens, for example, through social media.[12] However, it should be noted that although there are channels and efforts to listen to external stakeholders, it seems like this listening is merely about collecting data and not about genuine listening. It can be argued that there is a *transparent varnish*—organizations may appear to be listening, but in practice, the listening is about ticking the box: "we hear what you say but we are not interested in using what you say for development".

In the last chapter, we will discuss a management philosophy, the *service logic*, which we believe is an essential prerequisite for strategic listening. Service logic's strategic starting point is to be or develop into a customer-focused organization, which means adopting an outside-in perspective. Many organizations who start to listen to their customers genuinely may discover that their service proposition is not such a great salvation to humanity as they imagined. And it may turn out that customers have other needs or desires that are not being met by the organization's services and products.

Why Is Listening Important: Some Examples

- **Better conversations**—when a person speaking feels listened to, he or she will open up more and be more honest.
- **Increased trust and confidence**—a person who feels that they are listened to feels appreciated, has increased self-confidence, and feels greater trust in the person who listens.[13]
- **Increased job satisfaction and lower absenteeism**—are effects of genuine listening between managers and coworkers.
- **Higher productivity and quality of work**—listening has a clear relationship with higher productivity and higher quality of work. A person who listens is better able to learn from others and broaden their understanding. This, in turn, leads to better performance.
- **Increased sales**—when a salesperson listens to customers, the likelihood of closing, total sales volume, and quality of the sales presentation improve.[14]
- **Better relationships**—a listening manager has better relationships with his or her coworkers than a manager who does not listen. A salesperson who is perceived as a good listener by customers sells more.
- **More likable**—a good listener is more liked by the interlocutor. This is because a good listener is perceived as a caring person who shows an interest in people. This increases the feeling of trust.

The Forgotten Part of Communication

Listening is the *forgotten part of communication*.[15] At the same time, communication researchers have long stressed the importance of listening. As early as the late 1940s, Wilbur Schramm, who is seen as the founder of the American communication research, argued: "Listening is a powerful tool".[16]

Although it was already stated in 1940 that listening is a powerful tool in communication, we can unfortunately show in this book that it is a tool that is used too rarely and seems to be forgotten. The focus in most organizations' communication is generally to speak by sending out messages or information of various kinds. This is despite the fact that we know that listening has many benefits, such as you become a better speaker by listening since speaking and listening are linked. Or our blood pressure goes up when speaking and down when listening. Thus, there are even health reasons for becoming a better listener.

Listening to yourself is often seen as a positive thing. Feeling listened to helps us boost our self-esteem, as we get a feeling of being defined as necessary to others. Good listening is also a prerequisite for building strong relationships with other people. Those who are good listeners are liked by others.

Even though it is claimed that listening is a forgotten part in communication, we find that marketers have begun to argue for an increased focus on listening. There is less talk about researching or surveying the market, for example, via social media and instead more about "social media listening". In practice, social media listening means that organizations track, map, measure, and analyze online activities related to a particular product or brand.[17] Organizations that listen to their customers develop products and services based on how they use them, real needs, expectations, and desires. However, it still is an open question as to what extent this marketing method encompasses genuine listening. In the next chapter, we will discuss further what constitutes genuine listening.

There are several reasons why listening is strategically crucial for organizations. In the following chapters, we will further explain why listening is essential.

Welcome to the Fascinating World of Listening!

The listening research is unequivocal—listening in organizations has a tremendous and positive impact. Despite all the benefits of listening, as we mentioned at the beginning of this chapter, organizations are still mainly engaged in talking and disseminating information. More than 95 percent of organizational communication involves speaking, disseminating, or broadcasting information.[18] But looking at this positively means that organizations have enormous potential to develop strategic listening. The expression "Speech is silver, silence is gold" is thought to originate from the ancient Egyptians. Still, it was the German philosopher Thomas Carlyle who, in the mid-19th century, coined in print "Sprecfien ist silbern, Schweigen ist golden", which was later translated into English "If speech is silver, silence is gold".[19] We would like to modify the expression and state that *Speech is silver, listening is gold!* And we say welcome to the world of listening!

Speech is silver, listening is gold!

In the following chapters, we will discuss strategic communication and answer the following questions:

- What is it?
- Why is it important?
- How should it be fulfilled?

The more specific aim of this book is to increase knowledge about listening. To help organizations, as well as individuals, improve in strategic listening and, in doing so, help strengthen the listening skills of organizations and individuals.

A key message of this book is that organizations should work to design the organization for listening and systematizing practices that foster listening in the organization. Taking a more strategic approach to listening can ensure the engagement and motivation of the organization's stakeholders, increase their chances of success, and gain better long-term relationships with customers. We use the term "customer" for simplicity, but this term is not used by all organizations. Depending on the type of organization, your target group could be called patients, clients, citizens, or service users. When we use the term customer, all the different terms of whom we serve are included.

In this book, listening is allowed to get the attention it deserves to show the power and benefits of listening. This book offers no quick-fix *solutions* because we do not believe there are any. Listening is complex, and changing human listening behavior takes time and requires dedication. But how do you go about tackling and managing something complex? Desmond Tutu, archbishop of South Africa, is reputed to have said that there is only one way to eat an elephant: one bite at a time. By that, Tutu meant that anything that feels insurmountable and even impossible could only be dealt with by gradual evolution, one step at a time. This book therefore offers concrete tips and tools to help organizations and individuals gradually become better at listening and strategic listening.

Chapter 1

About Listening

LISTENING IN AN organizational context can be seen as something new and modern. But already in 1958, an article entitled "Listening to People" was published by Ralph G. Nichols and Leonard A. Stevens in *Harvard Business Review*. In the article, the researchers concluded that listening is the most critical component in organizational communication but also the weakest.[1] Although more than 60 years have gone by since this observation was made, not much has happened in this area. Listening is still neglected in many organizations, and whenever addressed in academic and popular literature on topics such as organizations, communication, leadership, and coworkers, listening is rarely the focus. All too often, listening is mentioned in passing. Whenever highlighted in the literature, it is mentioned as something extremely positive for organizations. But the lack of research on listening in communication and management theories could point to the fact that it seems to be taken for granted and as something entirely unproblematic.

In this chapter, we focus mainly on the listening of individuals and what listening in general means, while in Chapter 2, we look at the listening of organizations.

What Does Listening Mean?

We all understand, at least theoretically, what it means to listen. When we listen, we pay attention to what other people say. Ideally, we also reflect on what others are saying. When you really listen to someone, you comprehend not just the information—what is being said—but also the whole context in which the communication is taking place.[2] When we actually listen to someone, it is a way to build relationships. A relationship can be as short as a few minutes or a lifetime. Listening is, according to Carnegie, the best tool for creating and maintaining good relationships:

---

*What if there was a way to make all of your relationships better?
There is. It is called listening.*[3]

DOI: 10.4324/9781003413486-1

The listening that takes place in everyday life can be described as a cognitive process on a superficial level, although it is not active listening.[4] In practice, this means that we hear what is being said about a dilemma, a problem, a challenge, or a story about an experience, but too often we do not actively listen to what others tell us. In everyday life, we also tend not to listen to new ideas or feedback from the other person, even if that is what we want to do. This may be because active listening requires more attention and cognitive and behavioral effort.[5] This suggests that most of our communication in daily life is trivial and takes place entirely without any reflection. In this context, *responsiveness* may be worth mentioning, especially regarding leadership. Good or virtuous leadership is often linked in the academic literature and discourse to qualities such as coaching and responsiveness.[6] Many people confuse responsiveness with listening or use these terms synonymously. Responsiveness, however, is about a person's ability and sensitivity to perceive what is happening in a conversation—what it is about.[7] In other words, responsiveness is part of listening, but it is a broader concept.

Hearing and Listening

If we solely take in what other people say without reflecting or even caring about the content, we have engaged in hearing. It is therefore essential to distinguish between hearing and listening. Hearing can be described as a physical process that is relatively passive and that goes on all the time that we are awake.[8] Hearing is contrasted to listening, a mental and active process. Listening requires, first, that we *pay attention* and, second, that we *select* certain auditory stimuli while ignoring others.[9] In other words, auditory stimuli are sounds in our environment picked up by the outer ear and the external auditory canal in the form of sound waves. These are then transmitted to the eardrum, which is set in motion, and eventually, the signal reaches the brain's auditory cortex.

> ### Hearing and Listening[10]
>
> **Hearing** takes place unintentionally and automatically. It is what occurs when a sound vibration reaches the eardrum. We have all been in situations where we did not want to listen but could not avoid hearing, for example, sitting on a bus and unable to hear what the other passengers are talking about.
>
> **Listening** involves hearing and the process of trying to understand. It is a conscious activity that implies we successfully engage and participate in listening. It requires concentration and awareness to make sense of what others are saying.

Different Forms of Listening

It is also possible to distinguish between different forms of listening.[11] One form is called *mass listening*. An example of such listening is during a lecture or a speech at a large gathering. In mass listening, one person conveys information, and those attending the lecture listen and interact minimally. This form of listening has many similarities with the so-called *transmission view of* communication.[12] In this view, communication is understood as disseminating information through a medium, such as through direct speech or social media, from a sender, such as the management of an organization, to recipients. The assumption is that successful communication occurs when the recipient receives the information. Of course, this does not mean that the recipient understands or cares about the information. Many people listen without further interaction with the speaker, and the speaker does not know whether the listener understood the message. On the other hand, the speaker in front of an audience can understand whether what is being said evokes positive or negative emotions in the listener. By analyzing the body language, the speaker can see if people in the audience smile or look bored.

The second form of listening is *interpersonal listening*. It can take place face-to-face between two people who meet physically or be mediated through some medium such as a mobile phone or a videoconference. In an interpersonal context, such as in a meeting between colleagues or in a therapeutic conversation, interaction occurs all the time and the roles of speaker and listener shift during the conversation.[13] The goal of listening in an interpersonal context is to *understand* the other person, not to remember or store information, as is the case in a lecture.

In interpersonal listening, there is a continuous switch between being a speaker and a listener. These switches take place at lightning speed. In the role of listener, we use different behaviors to show that we are listening or are willing to listen. Two of the most common behaviors are *gaze* and *backchannelling*. By looking intently at the other person, we try to signal openness and willingness to listen. By responding with backchannelling, we show the speaker in different ways that we, as listeners, take a secondary role and are ready to listen. The backchannelling response was introduced as a concept by the professor of linguistics, Victor Yngve, and is part of basic human interaction.[14] These responses, such as humming or asking questions, enable us to have productive and meaningful interactions with other people. These two behaviors usually coincide—the listener looks intently at the other person while glancing back to show that he or she is still listening. Moreover, they happen unconsciously. But both are important to maintaining order and structure in who speaks and listens. Of course, situations may arise when one party does not accept being a listener and begins to compete for the role of speaker. The non-speaker begins to show she is uninterested in listening to the other.

Good Listening

When discussing listening, it often emerges that we all have experience with people who are more or less good at listening and that listening can be more or less effective. Therefore, it is also possible to talk about good listening. Research shows widespread beliefs about what we want others to *do* when they listen to us.[15] We also tend to tell people whether we think the other person has played the role of listener well or not. In addition, we are positively affected by someone who has been a good listener—good listening creates positive feelings.

Listen Actively

An example of good listening is often described as the listener being active and acknowledging the speaker. Good listening also means that the listener does not interrupt or try to influence the speaker. One might think that good listening is about "stroking the listener's hair" and agreeing with everything the person says. However, research suggests that this is not the case.[16] Instead, good listening is about us as listeners showing in different ways that we are active and *alert* and *giving feedback* to inform the speaker that we think what is being said is important and worth considering. Active listening was introduced as a concept by psychologists Carl R. Rogers and Richard E. Farson in the book *Active Listening*. It involved the listener giving the speaker free and undivided attention.[17] The active listener should try to understand what is being said based on her understanding of the world. It does not mean that we must agree with the other person, but when we engage in active listening, the goal is to better understand the other person's situation and perception. Through active, open, and unbiased listening, we are more likely to learn something new that may overturn our old beliefs.[18]

Researchers have often attempted to measure listener behavior objectively by collecting data through surveys. Recent research by Kriz, Kluger, and Lyddy shows that previous research has so far ignored examining how listeners perceive the *quality of listening*.[19] Their research shows that people feel listened to when the listener acts according to the speaker's expectations of the conversation. This means that when the listener pays attention to the speaker but later misses to follow up with expected actions, the speaker gets the feeling of being ignored. Furthermore, people do not feel listened to when the listener does not give a response, interrupts, or signals the end of the conversation. This leaves the speaker disappointed, and if no action is taken when the speaker gets the impression that something is about to happen, this is perceived as bad listening. However, Kriz and his colleagues emphasize that there is no expectation that the listener will act in a therapeutic conversation. Then, the expectations are only active listening and time set aside for listening.

The important thing is that when people feel that they are being listened to and understood, they experience a high degree of *intellectual humility* in the sense of daring to admit and showing that one may be wrong. The concept of intellectual humility was introduced by psychologist Julia M. Rohrer at the University of Leipzig, who, in her study, challenged fellow researchers to admit when they are wrong.[20] Björn Natthiko Lindeblad, a Swedish author and inspirer, wrote an autobiography called *I Can Be Wrong: And Other Wisdom from My Life as a Buddhist Monk*. He also argues how important it is to dare to admit that we all have flaws and sometimes make mistakes.[21] However, this is more difficult than one might think, not only for researchers but all people. We all find it hard to admit that we are wrong, and this is also made more difficult by the fact that in most contexts, cultures in general celebrate success, while mistakes and errors oftentimes are swept under the carpet. Thus, a culture that appreciates and honors those individuals who admit they are wrong and see this as material for development and learning is needed. In addition, we must be curious about our "blind spots" that prevent us from understanding everything. It has been found that people who are considered analytical intellectuals, such as researchers, have a tough time seeing these blind spots and admitting their mistakes.[22] This is because they have developed the ability to argue and defend their opinions. By being listened to, intellectual humility is trained and developed. People can then understand and realize their limitations and admit they may be wrong. When we get these insights that we are not always right, we have far better conditions to develop our listening skills and practice. Ultimately, listening is a skill that makes us more successful in life:

Among the basic skills we need for success in life, listening is primary.[23]

Good Listening According to Martin Buber

Martin Buber is considered one of the greatest contemporary philosophers. As a professor of religious studies and social philosophy, Buber is best known for his book *I and Thou*.[24] In his book, he laid the foundations for relational philosophy. According to Buber, we become individuals in our encounters with others. In the authentic encounter between "I" and "Thou", the other is not an object of experience. She is a subject who participates in the creation of "I", just as I participate in the creation of the "Thou".

In the book *I and Thou*, Buber suggests that the main thing in human life is the authentic encounter—the authentic conversation. Buber also argues that human beings have a remarkable ability to create relationships with others, not least through dialogue. Authentic encounters include listening as an essential part of becoming an individual.

According to Buber, listening involves active attention to the words and actions of the other and understanding them as explicitly directed at us. Mordechai Gordon, a professor of education, has analyzed Buber's view of listening and concludes that the relationship between speaking and listening is one of reciprocity and interdependence.[25] Gordon also stresses that, according to Buber, listening is vital in *creating a space* where two people can affirm each other as complete individuals. Listening, according to Buber, is about *being present* to the other.[26] In other words, listening is not just about learning different techniques or developing a specific listening skill. Good listening occurs when the listener is *psychologically ready* to listen and is present in the conversation. Hence, good listening occurs when we are present and open to the other person. At the same time, it is essential to point out that a prerequisite for good listening is mastering basic listening techniques (see more in the next chapter).

Furthermore, the practitioner of good listening has mastered the ability to:

- Show empathy for the speaker
- Be engaged in the conversation
- Be non-judgmental of the speaker
- Be respectful to the other

When open-minded and listening carefully to another person, you don't try to transfer your thoughts and ideas onto that person. Instead, it is about giving space for the person to create their understanding and meaning, which may differ from your own. Thus, good listening can imply giving space for sensemaking.

Bad Listening

The opposite of good listening is bad listening. There are, of course, many different types of bad listening. In conversations with others, we often feel disconnected because we filter out things that are said, that are not important to us. This can have severe consequences because bad listening, or the complete lack of listening, makes us feel lonely.[27] The feeling of loneliness is so great in our society that doctors talk about the loneliness epidemic. Instead, we listen to what we think is correct but don't try to understand what the other person is trying to convey. Furthermore, we view listening as simple and mundane but forget that active listening requires effort.

In the book *The Art of Communicating*, author Dale Ben Patterson lists six different forms of bad listening.[28] To become better listeners, we need to be aware of the different forms of bad listening to avoid them. Following we describe these six forms of bad listening.

Pseudo-Listening

When we communicate with others, we often feel we are having a dialogue. That is, we are talking *and* listening equally. Unfortunately, too often, we engage in *parallel monologues*.[29] This is a consequence of a lack of genuine interest in what others think and that we are rarely interested in changing our position. When a person gives the impression of listening but is thinking about something else or is not focused on genuine listening, it is a sign of *pseudo-listening*. This is a prevalent form of bad listening in situations where those who are expected to listen are obliged to. An example is when coworkers in an organization are forced to listen to a long speech from their immediate manager. Another example is students at a lecture who may appear to be listening but do not engage in active listening in practice. A further example may be when, during a conversation, a member of staff or a manager says: "I hear what you are saying". This may indicate a domination technique in not acknowledging the other person.[30] It could also be that the person has adopted a common management lingo learned from a leadership course. But what does the statement mean? Many of us who have received this response to what we have said probably feel that the person has noted what we have said but, in practice, ignores it. Of course, this harms the relationship because the person feels stupid and is more or less made to feel like an idiot. A final example of pseudo-listening is when organizations state that they are listening but only collect the information because it looks reasonable and rational. In other words, it is all about creating the right image. The fact that the image of managers and organizations sometimes is more important than actual actions was already recognized by the American historian Daniel Boorstin in 1962 in his book *The Image: A Guide to Pseudo-Events in America*.[31] In practice, the information gathered is rarely used to change decisions or strategies or develop new working methods, products, or services.[32] Rather, listening is done to portray the image of a listening organization or manager. Or simply because talking about listening is perceived as fancy or trendy.[33] The result of pseudo-listening, when the speaker(s) do not feel that they are being listened to, can be an increased resistance to the organization and various changes that have been decided upon. This can lead to disengagement, and coworkers become disloyal to the organization.[34]

Selective Listening

Another common form of bad listening is selective listening. It occurs when we, as listeners, only are interested in parts of a message that we find specific interest in. For example, when the chief executive officer (CEO) of a company has gathered all the coworkers to talk about the upcoming change process in the organization, most participants listen poorly only until their department is mentioned. Then suddenly, the department coworkers become particularly attentive and start listening with concentration.

Self-Centered Listening

A common barrier to listening is that we are too preoccupied with ourselves (see more later on barriers to listening). Self-centered listening means that we are primarily interested in getting our message across without really taking an interest in listening to see if the other person has something clever to say. New York–based comedian Fran Lebowitz allegedly said: "the opposite of talking isn't listening; the opposite of talking is waiting".[35] Lebowitz calls attention to the fact that often when we listen, we wait for the opportunity to speak to tell how we view or understand things, rather than actively listen to hear new perspectives or gain new experiences that may change our minds.

Fill-in-Listening

When we are or feel obliged to listen to someone, we may only listen selectively and to what we expect to hear. We may have an idea that the coworker we are talking to is not engaged in their work, and we only listen for signs of low engagement in their story. These are all examples of fill-in-listening. When something we are interested in or like comes up in the conversation, we try to fill in the previous messages that we have only been listening to inattentively. In this way, we build our own story and understanding around what the person has told us.

Isolated Listening

There are also times when we actively avoid listening. One example is in situations where what is being told makes us uncomfortable. It could be criticism of our work or our partner wanting to talk about how we are doing in our relationship. When we practice driving with our children and criticize them for how they drive, there is a good chance that they will stop listening. So instead of focusing on what it is in the message that should be listened to, all focus is put on avoiding taking the information in.

Defensive Listening

We hear things that have not been mentioned when we feel criticized and threatened. We interpret the critique as a criticism of ourselves as a person and that we are not good enough as we are rather than considering the criticism of the work. Defensive listening is typical in work life (between coworkers and between management and coworkers) and family life. Even a simple question could trigger defensive listening. An example is when a parent asks a teenager a question, and the teenager interprets it as if the parent does not trust them. And the other way around is also possible, when a similar question from the teenager may be perceived by the parent as a sign of disrespect.

> **Bad Listening Habits**[36]
> 1. When I focus too much on the person rather than the content
> 2. When I constantly interrupt the speaker
> 3. When I focus on details and miss the overall picture
> 4. When I force the other person's ideas to fit my mental models
> 5. When my body language signals a disinterest that creates uncertainty for the speaker
> 6. When I ignore what I don't understand and miss important or valid points
> 7. When I let my emotions get in the way and miss what is being said
> 8. When I daydream and am not fully present or actively listening

What Hinders Listening?

There are, of course, many things that hinder listening or even prevent it, such as the lack of communication channels for listening or an organizational culture that does not support listening. Many of these barriers stem from ourselves as individuals, such as our personalities, origins, feelings, experiences, and perceptions. Next we highlight some of the barriers documented in research on listening.

Focus on the Self

One of the most significant obstacles to listening in a conversation is self-centeredness. Most of the time, we listen not with the ambition to understand the other person but with the *desire to respond*.[37] The focus is on self-performance, and we are so preoccupied with talking to ourselves or preparing a response that we miss out on genuinely listening. By focusing on oneself, one's emotions, and the need to perform and appear suitable, the conditions for listening are weakened.[38] Humans are sometimes so preoccupied with ourselves and our thoughts that it hinders listening. Thus, if you want to listen, you need to let go of the focus on the self. The Swedish psychologist Margareta Berggren, who has long experience coaching managers, stresses:

Managers who want to engage in genuine dialogue need courage and personal development. It is not feasible to focus on the self and what one will gain from an action, but rather on what to find in common.[39]

It is challenging for many people to listen to others and let go of their self-centeredness. When we emanate from ourselves, we judge the other person based on our preconceptions or the values that guide us. One way to move away from this is to start with *empathic listening*. The American psychologist Marshall B. Rosenberg pioneered *non-violent communication*, also known as the giraffe language, to overcome many communication problems between people.[40] According to Rosenberg, people are unaware of their feelings, needs, and desires. Instead, people relate to the dominant norms of their culture. For example, how to be a boss, a coworker, a man, or a woman governs how we act and communicate with others. An essential part of the giraffe language is empathic listening. To engage in empathic listening, you must let go of yourself and your judgments and try to see reality from the other person's eyes. Only then can empathic listening be achieved. It means trying to walk in the other person's shoes for a while and putting yourself in the eyes of the other. Psychologist Daniella Gordon advises: "Allow yourself to be moved and changed by what you hear".[41]

Hard to Listen to Yourself

While the sections earlier describe self-centeredness as an obstacle to listening, previous research also highlights the problem that people find it hard to listen to themselves. How should we understand this? The barrier stems from the fact that people need to show themselves the same respect that they expect others to show. Showing yourself respect is important, as it frees up energy to increase your engagement in listening to others.[42] When we don't have self-respect, we are harsh to ourselves and may think we are not worth loving.

There are no *quick fixes* to repair poor self-respect. Anyone who feels that they do not have enough self-respect could need support from a therapist. Working with a therapist to develop yourself and self-respect is a good investment that will allow you to grow. We would argue that all people could benefit and develop from therapy. We all have different fears and "choppiness" that we must deal with to feel better. However, too many people might fear therapy or psychologists—they may think the psychologist will "reveal" innermost thoughts that should be kept secret. Of course, this is not the case; this is an unfounded fear. A psychologist is usually a master listener and can help you reflect on fears and perceived short-comings and provide thinking tools and exercises to strengthen self-respect.

Fear

We are all afraid of different things and different situations. Fear is the most vital human emotion since it can help us avoid dangerous situations. The fear we feel is a sense of anxiety about something we perceive as a threat. The threat can be both real and perceived. For example, speaking in front of a group of people is not dangerous, but we can still strongly perceive it as a threat and feel afraid.

Although fear is often a good emotion that can save us in certain situations, it also causes problems for people. Fear is one reason many people in organizations find it challenging to listen to others. It can be a perceived fear of being criticized, appearing weak, not having the answers or being unable to act, and so forth. Further, fear makes us not listen because we are afraid of being challenged in one way or another. In addition, listening to people talk about bad experiences can also be challenging and demanding. As a listener, you must deal with and endure the heavy emotions that can arise.

Anyone who wants to improve their listening should try to work with their personal development to acknowledge their shortcomings and patterns. Basically, all people have different kinds of fear, and we need to reflect on that and try to understand why we become afraid. American sociologist Brené Brown has spent two decades studying fear and vulnerability. In her book *Dare to Lead*, Brown stresses that one of the main problems in organizations is managers who avoid difficult conversations and giving feedback. The consequences are lack of clarity, loss of trust and commitment, and passive-aggressive behavior.[43] Brown explains that managers' reluctance to communicate and listen is due to fear and not daring to show vulnerability. If managers in organizations had shown themselves to be more vulnerable, and therefore more human, internal trust would increase. Former SAS CEO Jan Carlzon reflects on his professional life in his book *Se människan!* [*Eng.* See the Human!]. Carlzon underlines that over the years, he learned that no coworker expected him to know everything or to be the best or to have complete control.[44] At the beginning of his career, he imagined that there were expectations for him to have all the answers. But over the years, he realized the power of showing vulnerability and not always having all the answers to problems. This made it possible for his coworkers to grow.

Expectation of Action

There is a concern that listening *can create expectations for action* that one does not feel they have the power or ability to carry out. These expectations to act and solve problems make people avoid listening. In the short term, avoiding listening may feel like an effective strategy to avoid the extra work and possible anxiety that acting on these expectations may entail. Many managers, therefore, avoid listening to their coworkers.

Initial Occurrence Syndrome

In psychology, the term *initial occurrence syndrome* is used to explain what prevents us from listening. It is a syndrome that entails that we mainly absorb information that is most available in our memory or that has been experienced in the past.[45] This means we find listening difficult when we hear things we have not experienced before. Accordingly, we turn off our listening. The syndrome explains why both coworkers and management reject and distrust information that they do not recognize. Instead of listening, it is easy to start defending what we already know quickly and already have experience with in the past.

Confirmation Bias

Another phenomenon that is linked to initial occurrence syndrome is *confirmation bias*. Nobel laureate Daniel Kahneman and his colleague Amos Tversky have shown that humans have a strong confirmation bias that makes us willing to seek out or listen to information that confirms what we already know and believe to be true.[46] This phenomenon is further fueled by filter bubbles and opinion corridors. Thus, we tend to pay attention to and take in information that supports our views. These can give rise to tunnel vision and arise, inter alia, in and through social media. Following we have listed some of the most common examples of confirmation bias that we are sure many of us can relate to.

Examples of How Confirmation Bias Occurs

- When we are not looking for objective facts
- When we interpret information to support our beliefs
- When we only remember details that enforce our beliefs
- When we ignore information that does not support what we believe

Confirmation bias and opinion corridors are also explanations for *functional stupidity* in organizations, i.e., managers and coworkers doing what is expected of them without thinking or reflecting on whether it is good.[47] It is too rare for organizations to stop and reflect on actions or decisions and hence avoid functional stupidity. Many times it is argued that "we've always done it this way", "everyone else does it", "our policies say", and "our procedures mean".

Interestingly, people with high intelligence in the traditional sense, i.e., being good at logical and abstract thinking, easily fall victim to confirmation bias.[48] Many managers are considered to have high intelligence, which means they are better at convincingly explaining their mistakes to themselves and others. This, in turn, leads them to become more and more dogmatic in their beliefs. This also rubs off on the organization's coworkers, who are less likely to stop and reflect on, for example, the organization's policies and procedures. The organization then becomes what Mats Alvesson, professor of business administration, calls *functional stupidity*. The only way to avoid this trap is for managers to become aware of their confirmation bias and try to act differently than usual. It is also essential not to take hypotheses and thoughts about how things are too severely.[49] If one is too attached to their original beliefs, they may find it difficult to let them go even if new information comes to light that points in a different direction and reveals that the initial answer was wrong. John Coleman, who wrote the article "Critical Thinking Is About Asking Better Questions", published in *Harvard Business Review*, suggests that we should view our initial responses to beliefs as "straw men". Making a straw man means attributing to someone an opinion that the person does not hold or formulating envy of their opinion and then criticizing the opinion. It becomes easier to drop the first response if new information that requires a new response comes to light.

Summary

- When you genuinely listen, you focus not just on the information but the overall situation where communication is taking place.
- Distinguish between listening that takes place unintentionally and listening that is a conscious activity that requires commitment to succeed.
- Good listening takes place when the listener is active and acknowledges the speaker.
- Bad listening takes place when we focus primarily on ourselves and are not interested in learning something new or changing our mind.
- Common barriers to listening are self-centeredness, fear, and confirmation bias.

Chapter 2

Strategic Listening

IN THE PREVIOUS chapter, we focused on individuals' listening. In this chapter, we will look at listening in an organizational setting. We discuss what strategic listening entails and how we can understand the concept of strategic listening. We will also present a range of reasons why it is essential for organizations to listen strategically. We begin the chapter by noting that successful organizations do listen.

Successful Organizations Listen

Plenty of research shows a strong link between listening and successful organizations. Attempts have been made to calculate in monetary terms how much it costs organizations *not* to engage in listening and what the benefits of increased listening can be. However, these calculations are complex and tend only to be pure speculations. But research has also measured the impact of listening in qualitative terms, some of which we have already mentioned in previous chapters. Later in this chapter, we will discuss a range of reasons why organizations should listen and the qualitative benefits that can arise, such as fewer sick days and greater engagement.

The importance of listening for organizations was featured in research as early as the late 1950s.[1] Listening continued to interest researchers in the 1960s and 1970s, but it was not until the 1980s that the importance of listening became more widely known. It was through Tom Peters and Robert Waterman's *In Search of Excellence*, one of the best-selling management books of all time, that managers around the world were able to learn that the most successful organizations are good at listening.[2] In the so-called excellent organizations, customers are listened to and prioritized, and management, as well as executives, listen to their coworkers. The result of listening is that the organization can adapt more quickly to changes in the market, avoid crises, streamline learning, strengthen relationships, increase engagement, and so on:

> *The most successful companies are not only better at service, quality, reliability, and finding a niche. They are better listeners.*[3]

DOI: 10.4324/9781003413486-2

Listening Crisis

Although it has long been known that successful organizations listen, few organizations devote enough time to it or take listening seriously. We know that listening can be difficult for many people. It is difficult for managers and coworkers in organizations to truly listen to each other and various stakeholders such as customers, politicians, interest groups, etc.

Australian researcher Jim Macnamara was one of the earliest to take an interest in organizational listening and has written several articles and reports in this field of research. Macnamara also wrote one of the first books in the field—*Organizational Listening: The Missing Essential in Public Communication*.[4] Macnamara argues that organizations generally do not pay enough attention to listening and that this is a major crisis.[5] According to Macnamara, organizations listen sporadically, often poorly, and sometimes not at all.[6] The crisis can be partly explained by the fact that listening often is seen as something that both individuals and organizations take for granted. Macnamara argues that a change is needed—a turnaround that directs more significant attention to listening. Organizations need to listen more to their stakeholders and coworkers and continually adapt their strategy based on what they hear. Stop treating listening as a secondary issue and elevate this vital activity to its rightful place. Listening is thus a central part of organizational communication and should be viewed as equally important as voice and speech.

As previously mentioned, a challenge for many organizations is pseudo-listening. Pseudo-listening occurs when someone pretends to listen but, in practice, does not. A similar phenomenon but related to dialogue is referred to as *quasi-dialogue*. Managers and executives may say that they want to have an ongoing dialogue with coworkers. However, as they hear what is being said, they do not actively listen. A comprehensive UK study of more than 2,000 coworkers indicated that pseudo-listening was expected and that many coworkers were afraid to make their voices heard or voice criticism within the organization.[7] This kind of listening is problematic because it risks eroding trust between managers and coworkers. Thus, a positive internal climate is one of the most critical factors for a well-functioning organization.

Pseudo-listening also occurs concerning external groups, such as customers, citizens, and users. It is common nowadays for customers to be offered to answer a survey or to be called after using an organization's service. This is an example of the feedback culture that has emerged as a standard model and can be explained by the extensive reliance on measurability in quantitative terms. As Imran Rashid points out in his book *Feelability*,[8] it is also one of the reasons why we humans feel stressed, pressured, and depressed. Philosopher Jonna Bornemark also agrees with this, and she highlights that we live in an age of measurability. Therefore, we constantly try to control reality and solve problems by measuring and quantifying.[9]

Causes of Poor Listening by Organizations

In the report "Organizational Listening in Public Communication: Emerging Theory and Practice", Jim Macnamara has compiled ten years of research on organizational listening.[10] The report is based on an extensive survey of 60 organizations on three continents, with 300 interviews and a large amount of text analysis, including social media posts. Macnamara found ten various reasons why organizations are bad at listening. Following, we have listed seven reasons that we believe are of particular importance for organizations to know about:

1. *Arrogant culture and elitism.* In many organizations, there is a culture of arrogance and elitism within management. Frequently, leaders believe they have access to enough knowledge to make adequate decisions. Coworkers', customers', and other target groups' opinions are dismissed and not recognized as important or significant.

2. *Transmission view of communication.* This view of communication leads the organization to engage primarily in various campaigns where it can tell others how it views things. Thus, there is a bias towards one-way communication, while two-way communication is neglected.

3. *Quantitative surveys.* Most of the market and social research carried out by organizations comprises quantitative surveys. These are important for generalizing results and identifying averages. However, qualitative surveys are also needed to explore people's feelings easier and better understand how people understand and perceive things. It is crucial to understand people's emotions, as they can explain a lot about people's behavior.

4. *The wrong starting point for engagement with stakeholders.* Too often, organizations' engagement and relationships with stakeholders are premised on the goal of informing and persuasion rather than on a mutual exchange where meaning can be co-created.

5. *Collaboration as ritual.* Public consultations are often just rituals that take place because it looks good instead of the organization listening to its stakeholders. Organizations may tick the box that they have listened to stakeholders without genuine interest in receiving new thoughts or ideas that can develop the organization and its business.

6. *The usual suspect.* When organizations provide opportunities for communication and listening practices with stakeholders, they usually make various professionals attend with a particular or special interest in the issue to be discussed. This gives the organization too narrow of a perspective on the issue and does not gather a broader and more varied view.

7. *Social media for dissemination of messages.* Most organizations use social media as another channel to deliver their messages to different target audiences rather than as a two-way communication and listening medium.

The reasons suggested, in addition to several other reasons why organizations are bad at listening, also mean that organizations miss out on opportunities to gain the many positive values that listening can bring (see, for example, the box in the introductory chapter).

Consequences of Not Listening

There are plenty of examples of what can happen when organizations listen poorly, pseudo-listen, or do not listen to their coworkers and customers. The most drastic ones involve organizations going bankrupt or entering a crisis with reduced sales, trust, and legitimacy.

In cases where the organization has failed to listen to its customers and adopted a "bottom-up" perspective, this may have resulted in the launch of new services or products not being successful in the market—customers are not interested. It may be that customers have not demanded the new product or that market preferences have changed. When an organization has a traditional inside-out perspective rather than an outside-in perspective that focuses on the customer experience, it may be that managers and coworkers in the organization have overconfidence that the service or product is superior and of more excellent value to the customer.

The Facit Case

The case of the Swedish company Facit is a classic example of when listening did not occur. The company became the world's leading manufacturer of electronic calculators during the Second World War and peaked in the late 1960s, with 14,000 coworkers in 140 countries. Since 1957, turnover has increased by 500 percent. In the early 1970s, the company faced a severe financial crisis with rapidly declining profits. At a time when management had just invested heavily in expanding production facilities, digitization took hold. Electronic calculators from Japan, which were cheaper and more straightforward, quickly became a threat to Facit. The management ignored this advancement because they were convinced of the outstanding product the company was producing. But time caught up with the company, and Electrolux bought Facit in 1972.

The Toyota Case

The case of the Japanese car company Toyota is another example of when listening was not successful. As Toyota has a long tradition of focusing on high quality and safety, it also has an excellent reputation for the quality of its cars. However, for several years Toyota has had to recall many of its cars due to malfunctioning brakes. Since 2009, Toyota has recalled 7.1 million cars in at least three rounds. This could probably have been avoided if management had listened to coworkers who repeatedly reported the problem. Japanese companies are known for listening to their coworkers and working with them to identify, avoid, and manage problems. For a long time, Toyota also established an organization for listening to its customers to improve the quality of its cars. However, something happened to Toyota and its capacity to listen to coworkers and customers. One explanation is that the established standards, norms, values, and organizational culture were "forgotten" over time due to the increased pressure from new managers with new agendas as well as owners' desire to increase profit in stiffening competition.[11] Toyota had a well-functioning listening culture. Still, listening began to be taken for granted and then forgotten, especially by management. In other words, it is vital to ensure that the listening culture is maintained by management. Listening occurs, and management considers and uses the information retrieved from coworkers, customers, and other stakeholders.

The BlackBerry Case

A further example of an organization that did not engage in strategic listening is the case of BlackBerry. The Canadian company was among the first to launch smartphones. At its peak in the summer of 2009, the company had half of the US market, but by 2014 its market share had dropped to 1 percent. Adam Grant, author of the book *Think Again*, says that one of the reasons for BlackBerry's downfall was that its founder and CEO Mike Lazaridis was responsible for all product and technical decisions within the company.[12] Lazaridis is a genius who, as a teenager, had already developed several successful inventions. Although his innovative solutions led to the first smartphones, the company could not adapt to market changes. Lazaridis was convinced that he knew what product customers needed and, according to Grant, found it hard to rethink. It may be added that neither Lazaridis as CEO nor the company as an organization was good at strategic listening.

Strategic listening is not only about listening and obtaining information, opinions, thoughts, and feelings but also about reflecting, thinking, evaluating, and possibly adjusting opinions while making new decisions. In an article in *The Global and Mail*, one coworker says the problem was not that they stopped listening to customers. The problem was that managers and coworkers in the company were convinced that they knew more about what customers needed long before they knew it themselves. At the same time, this is a tricky balancing act, as there have been examples of companies that developed products and services and addressed needs that the customers did not realize they had. Examples of such services are Spotify and Swish.

Take Listening Seriously!

To avoid the failures described in the cases earlier, a new strategic approach to listening is called for. Listening is central to the ability of organizations to cope with the complexity and speed of change in the world that surrounds them. It involves listening to stakeholders such as customers, and it involves listening to coworkers who have the expertise, experience, feelings, and knowledge that are important for various strategic decisions. This means, among other things, designing and developing the organization for more *strategic listening*. A strategic approach means that listening needs to be practiced in and by the whole organization—such as between coworkers, managers and coworkers, management and coworkers, and customers and coworkers. Customer service, salespeople, innovation units, and communicators may have a particularly important role in listening, but so do other coworkers, most minor managers, and senior management. But it is also about designing internal processes, digital technologies, and other resources for listening. In other words, strategic listening affects everyone in the organization and requires everyone to try to become better listeners. It is simply a matter of taking listening seriously!

About Strategic Listening

If we want to go a bit more thorough with the term, what exactly is strategic listening? If we start by searching for strategic listening in the research databases of university libraries (e.g., EBSCO), we do not get many hits. When we searched for the term at the end of 2022, we only received 22 hits. Extending the search to the related term organizational listening yielded 25 hits. Out of these, most are related to the field of pedagogy: articles that describe how students can develop their listening skills more effectively by formulating their questions better. If the search is reduced to listening and organization, 117 articles published since 2000 are found.[13] A literature review of these articles shows that research on listening in an organizational context is fragmented and occurs in subjects such as management, psychology, and communication, which all have different theoretical and methodological starting points.[14]

There are also not many books that take an organizational perspective on listening. Only two international books focus on strategic and organizational listening (except for the book you are reading now). One book, *The Power of Strategic Listening*, is written by communications professor Laurie Lewis.[15] The book is about how organizations can become better listeners, and Lewis concludes that better interpersonal listening skills are needed. In other words, managers and coworkers need to become better at listening to individuals from different backgrounds and contexts. The book also offers a framework for how organizations can build and establish a listening culture, structure, and practices to support strategic listening. The second book, mentioned earlier, is *Organizational Listening* by Jim Macnamara.[16] The book challenges organizations' common claim that they are interested in two-way communication and dialogue. Based on a two-year research project on three continents, Macnamara found that organizations generally listen poorly, sporadically, and often not at all. Macnamara offers a listening architecture model that describes several elements that make up organizational listening. We will discuss Lewis and Macnamara's models in Chapter 7, which we believe are great starting points but lack some crucial elements.

To succeed in defining strategic listening, we must begin by focusing on two words—strategic and listening. In the sections that follows, we first discuss the two concepts of strategy and listening before moving on to the definition of strategic listening.

About Strategy

Strategy is one of the most broadly explored areas in management research. As a result, much has been written about strategy in both popular and academic literature. As no unambiguous definition of strategy exists, it is somewhat unclear what strategy means. However, what unites most views of strategy is that it is about how to make an organization successful.[17] In this book, we will just briefly point out the main lines of strategy research.

Historically, strategy is linked to the art of war in how generals plan to win wars.[18] In organizations, strategy is often used as a term for a plan on how the organization will deal with the future and be successful. A traditional view of strategy in research is that the strategic plan should provide information about where the organization is going and how to get there. Strategy is therefore seen as a rational process in which managers gather all available and objective information, thoroughly analyze it, and use it to draw up a detailed plan.[19] The strategy thus consists of a plan describing actions to achieve the set objectives. However, strategy is often seen as something that heroic and forceful managers in a boardroom develop. Moreover, the traditional view of strategy has been criticized for presuming that the world stands still and does not change when the strategic plan is implemented.

The traditional view of strategy as a linear formulation and implementation process has now been replaced by a more dynamic and process-oriented view.[20] One of the creators of this newer approach is the American strategy researcher Henry Mintzberg, who observed managers[21] and strategic decision-making[22] as early as the 1970s. Mintzberg was able to show that decision-making and strategies in practice were not nearly as rational as the traditional normative models advocated. Instead, Mintzberg argues that managers' decision-making usually is unstructured. The un-structuredness is particularly evident in complex situations with no optimal solution.

Being strategic is about dealing with ambiguous situations, i.e., there are no given and ready answers.[23] Strategy can therefore be described as a form of problem-solving. However, solving a problem one does not grasp or understand is impossible. It is therefore a matter of trying to describe how the problem is perceived and the ability to focus and refine the problem so that it becomes tangible—the hallmark of a good strategist.[24]

The traditional view of strategy assumes that there is an objective world that can be described. However, the process-oriented view claims that only a socially constructed reality exists. In other words, we interpret information in different ways depending on our background, interests, culture, etc., and create a particular understanding from which we act.[25] In a classic article from 1985, "Strategic Management in an Enacted World", Linda Smircich and Charles Stubbart write that managers should "think more about how they learned what they know and think less about what they know".[26] In other words, managers should see themselves as creators of a world they act upon through strategy rather than adapting the organization's strategy to an objective reality. Hence, what is needed for successful leadership is more reflexivity.

Strategic decisions need to be made in new, complex situations where given answers are lacking. The well-known professor of organizational psychology, Karl E. Weick, argues that an essential part of acting strategically is the ability to improvise at the moment.[27] According to Weick, we cannot rely on old models of thinking, traditions, or tools when faced with a new and complex situation. We need to act to understand; afterward, when we have acted, we can better make sense of what we are witnessing. Thus, acting strategically is very much about acting in the situation and improvising. However, improvising requires solid knowledge and a supportive organizational culture with norms and values that help us choose how to act. Therefore, an organization needs to have explicit norms and values and managers and coworkers need to have actively discussed and elaborated on their meaning and importance.

To summarize the research on strategy, researchers today focus less on how strategies are developed by managers or how these are implemented in the organization and more on how strategies are realized by coworkers. Strategy is in this sense seen as a verb—*strategizing*—the making of strategy.[28] Paula Jarzabkowiski, one of the leading researchers behind the *strategy-as-practice* research tradition, and her colleagues argue that previous research on strategy has missed the processes and actions that can be strategic in their nature and action but are not predetermined strategic.[29] Researchers are interested in how multitudes of micro-actions by coworkers lead to a strategic, aggregate outcome. This approach to strategy means that even staff who are not usually considered to be working strategically, such as telemarketers, customer and contact center staff, and nurses, are in practice working strategically, and their work has a strategic effect. In other words, researchers and those working in organizations may miss the critical indirect strategic actions that can have large aggregate and positive effects. Consequently, strategy is not something an organization has but something coworkers in organizations *do*.[30] This means that strategic listening is ultimately about having a plan, a management philosophy, that puts listening and how listening is realized in the organization as a priority.

The Concept of Listening

In the previous chapter, we discussed listening but did not define the term. There are, of course, many proposed definitions of listening, but despite over a hundred years of research, there is no universally accepted definition.[31] D.S. Mower, a professor of philosophy, argues that listening is a continuous activity that is usually goal-oriented and is always capable of improvement.[32] In an extensive literature review on interpersonal listening, communication researchers Lipetz, Kluger, and Bodie found that listening has three dimensions: cognitive, behavioral, and emotional.[33]

- *The cognitive dimension*, i.e., the thinking dimension of listening, is often described as "listening with understanding",[34] receiving and interpreting,[35] and showing curiosity and interest.[36]

- *The behavioral dimension* of listening allows the speaker to understand that listening is taking place. It involves both verbal and non-verbal behavior.
- *The emotional dimension* consists of three parts. The most crucial part is empathic listening, leading to an emotional response that allows one to understand the feelings of the other. The second part is inclusion, which is about respecting and accepting others as they are. The third and final part of the emotional dimension is supportive, often described as the primary means of helping others to develop and create a sense of security and support. When listening works well with, for example, a close friend, a priest, a psychologist, or a boss, the person who is telling feels safe and can tell the story openly without putting up any defense.

In conclusion, listening is actively paying attention to what others say.

Definitions of Strategic Listening

Strategic listening is about goal-oriented listening fulfilled to achieve a given goal. Based on the research on strategy, we can conclude that strategic listening is both about having *knowledge of listening strategies* and *being able to use these* strategies.[37] Strategic listening can be described as a flexible process of being aware of how listening works; having a set of appropriate listening strategies in different contexts; and planning, investigating, and evaluating after listening.[38]

As previously mentioned, Macnamara describes organizational listening as a composite of different organizational elements, such as culture, policies, structures, skills, techniques, and practices used to listen to organizations' stakeholders.[39] Macnamara has emphasized that organizations that want to be both democratic and ethical listen to their stakeholders and that this builds trust and reputation. On the other hand, Lewis emphasizes the importance of the internal perspective and how coworkers and managers should work to listen strategically.[40] Lewis points out that it is usually not the organizations' willingness to listen to stakeholders that is the problem. Instead, the problem is that many organizations do not have the processes to act on the information they receive through listening. Thus, many organizations engage in pseudo-listening rather than listening actively and acting on what is being said. Rather than just ticking the box that the organization engages in listening, many organizations need to be better at dealing with information that does not confirm what is liked and has been decided in the organization. Managers need to question fundamental assumptions better and make real organizational changes. Lewis emphasizes that the overall goal of strategic listening is to bring up what was previously unknown, to question what is usually taken for granted, and to challenge the dominant norms or beliefs of managers and units in the organization to ensure that wise decisions are made.

Laurie Lewis offers the following definition of strategic listening:

> Strategic organizational listening is a set of methods and structures designed and used to ensure that an organization's attention is focused on critical information and inputs to enable learning, questioning key assumptions, making better decisions, and ensuring self-critical analysis.[41]

We agree with Lewis's definition of strategic listening, but we would like to offer a slightly simplified definition that we believe is easier to use and put into practice.

Our Definition of Strategic Listening

STRATEGIC LISTENING is the relationship-oriented, goal-oriented, and systematized listening of organizations that creates the conditions for successful operations.

Strategic listening requires a management that focuses on listening when organizing, leading, and controlling the business.

Strategic listening makes demands on organization, management, governance, and training.

The Dark Side of Strategic Listening

Listening is generally associated with something positive. But, as always, we should be aware that listening can have a darker side. Listening can be harmful, as can be the case when it is associated with surveillance. For example, such listening, or rather the surveillance that the East German secret police Stasi carried out against citizens through their massive wiretapping activities, exemplifies the strategic listening that is negative. Another example is the Chinese Ministry of State Security (Guoanbu), which has a gigantic activity of listening to Chinese citizens and others using artificial intelligence (AI), among others. Another example of listening from a negative perspective is some of the surveillance on social media. In her book *The Age of Surveillance Capitalism*, Shoshana Zuboff describes how the internet's dissemination of information is increasingly becoming a large-scale industry where people, customers, and citizens are being monitored.[42] Zuboff describes in detail how Google, Facebook, Apple, and Amazon, among others, engage in surveillance, collecting information about users that is then sold to other actors without people's knowledge. This can be seen as a negative form of listening.

Two Forms of Professional Listening

In an organizational context, there are different forms of professional listening. It can be helpful to think about which form of listening is essential and to be clear about why you are engaging in one form or another. One form can be called *knowledge-oriented listening* and is used when you want to gather more information to develop new knowledge on which to base decisions. This may involve acting in a certain way to avoid a crisis, developing new products or services, or gaining more knowledge about changing customer preferences. The second form of listening can be called *confirmatory listening* and is not primarily used instrumentally to gather information, but to confirm the other person. Here the aim is to make the other person feel important, heard, seen, and acknowledged. While the former is adjusted towards generating new knowledge, the latter is geared towards strengthening relationships, making people feel appreciated and necessary, and thereby increasing engagement.

Two Forms of Professional Listening

Knowledge-Oriented Listening

Goal: Acquire information and produce new knowledge
Requirement: Be prepared to change your position
Model: Listen → Collect → Assess and analyze → Act → Feedback

Confirmatory Listening

Goal: Create better relationships and make others feel appreciated ("seen and heard")
Requirement: Set aside time and be present at the moment
Model: Listen → Be a resource for the other → Affirm the other

Why Should Organizations Listen Strategically?

In any organization, there is great potential for increasing strategic listening. By listening to coworkers with a wealth of knowledge, intuition, emotion, experience, networks, and a feel for how the organization is doing, the organization can adapt more quickly to change. Customers, or those outside the organization, have lots of thoughts, ideas, and experiences that are important for the organization to listen to so as to better meet the expectations and needs of its stakeholders. In strategy research, there is talk of opening the strategy process, which means including more people both inside and outside the organization (for example, partners and customers) in the development of new strategies.[43] In other words, including more people in the strategy process requires increased strategic listening to coworkers, customers, or other stakeholders, increasing organizations' external and internal trust.

When listening is addressed and discussed in scholarly texts on organizations and management, it is rarely listening that is the main focus.[44] A clear pattern in research on listening in organizations is to show that good listening leads to increased sales or customer satisfaction. Another pattern is that effective listening is linked to objective measures such as improved individual and organizational performance. For example, one study found that clients who rated their financial advisor highly on the ability to listen had higher trust in the advisory firm and experienced greater satisfaction with the service.[45] They are also more likely to continue to purchase the firm's services regularly. A further example of the power of listening is taken from a study in the healthcare sector. In an American study, researchers examined the relationship between doctors' communication and the number of lawsuits filed against the doctor.[46] The research shows that primary care physicians who have not received any lawsuits from patients spend more time on each patient visit, more than three minutes extra time on each visit. The explanation is probably that patients felt seen, listened to, and recognized as individuals. This goes well in hand with Martin Buber's view of listening, which we discussed previously in this chapter. Other research shows that if coworkers perceive widespread listening in the organization, it positively impacts its sales and bottom line.[47] A third pattern in the research is that listening is seen as a skill that can be practiced and developed, and even small efforts can positively affect the organization's performance.[48]

In conclusion, all the research shows unequivocally that listening has a significant and positive impact on organizations, such as increased profitability and better ability to face crises and manage change.[49] Following, we delve into three reasons why organizations should engage in strategic listening to improve:

- Leadership
- Coworker relations
- Relationships with stakeholders

Listening for Better Leadership

Strategic listening is closely linked to modern leadership models such as value-based leadership and trust-based management. Modern leadership focuses less on the manager and his or her importance and more on the importance of coworkers and customers in creating value. In other words, by strategic listening, we do not mean listening that "strategically" merely "picks the information" that confirms what we already like, have decided on, or have perceived as usual. Topical research shows unequivocally that managers who spend little time listening to others reduce organizational effectiveness, whereas a manager who shows emotion and listens clearly improves coworker performance.[50] Trust-based management, distributed leadership, and value-based leadership are ideals and models used in many organizations today. They are based on empowering coworkers to make decisions based on shared values and trust. These decentralized models require active listening from both leaders and coworkers, as well as active listening to other stakeholders.[51]

At the same time, it is interesting to note that in research on organizations and leadership, listening has received little attention. In modern research on trust-based leadership, little is mentioned about the value of listening in building trust.[52] It is mentioned merely fleetingly or not at all. This may seem odd, as much research shows that listening is central to developing trust in organizations. We will return to leadership and listening in Chapter 5.

Listening for Better Coworkership

Engaged and motivated coworkers are the foundation of a successful organization. This, in turn, requires a listening organization where coworkers feel seen and listened to. A person who feels listened to is both active and engaged. Research shows that the relationship between listening and job satisfaction and engagement is much stronger than with other well-known factors such as pay and job content.[53] This relationship is not well known because both organizations and management training sometimes focus too much on the importance of other factors, such as motivation and pay, in creating engagement rather than teaching managers the art of listening.

There is also a clear connection between listening and creativity. Previous studies show that if managers in an organization are good listeners, there is a sense of psychological safety among coworkers.[54] This psychological safety allows coworkers to dare to try new ideas, fail, and sometimes succeed. In such a process, there is a good chance that new creative and innovative solutions will emerge.

Many organizations become functionally stupid because internal listening happens far too seldom.[55] Through strategic listening, learning is fostered, and wise organizations can evolve. By actively listening to coworkers, organizations can harness the power of coworker expertise and experience. We return to coworker leadership and listening in Chapter 6.

Listening for Better Stakeholder Relations

Modern leadership takes an outside-in perspective, putting the customer's value creation at the center rather than a traditional inside-out perspective. With a traditional perspective on organization and management, it is too often assumed that the organization alone has the solution to the customer's problems with the services and products offered. Taking an outside-in perspective, referred to in services research as "*service logic*", requires the organization to listen to the customers to develop both products and services that are of value to customers. Even within the organization, modern leadership is based on dialogue and listening. Consequently, contemporary leadership requires a much greater *focus on listening*.

Modern service research shows that value is created together with customers. Co-creating value requires actively listening to those that the organization serves. Many of the problems experienced by customers could quickly be addressed if managers and coworkers spent more time listening to customers.[56] Browne and Nuttall argue that:

Organizations spend most of their time trying to convince audiences that they are correct, rather than listening to the problems and needs of stakeholders.[57]

Successful organizations have good relationships with and a high level of trust among coworkers, customers, users, citizens, politicians, journalists, and other stakeholders.[58] This has also been demonstrated repeatedly in research. Good trust creates more effective and successful organizations.[59] Trust between the organization and its stakeholders is often built through good customer relations. If coworkers acknowledge customers so they feel seen and heard, trust will improve and strengthen the relationship. This lays the foundations for long-term relationships, which have a variety of benefits, not least financial, as it is more cost-effective to have customers who know the organization and can easily navigate its processes.

By actively listening to and sharing information, views, ideas, opinions, and experiences, organizations can better adapt quickly to current or changing circumstances. For example, coworkers with direct customer contact, such as in a customer center or other customer-facing functions, get early signals about when something is not working or when customers like or dislike what the organization does or offers. Despite the customer-facing staff's wealth of knowledge, they are only sometimes seen as a critical resource for information, learning, and decision-making.

Service innovation usually involves customers and coworkers in generating new thoughts and ideas that can lead to innovation. Many of the best innovations have emerged thanks to co-creation between coworkers and customers. To ensure that both stakeholders' knowledge and experience are brought to bear on the organization, they must be listened to. The problem is often that this does not work because there needs to be an open communication climate and an understanding of the importance of strategic listening.[60] As customers usually know better what they need than the organization does, listening to them can be an effective way to innovate.

Research also shows that many contentious issues and large organizational crises could have been avoided if organizations had devoted more time to strategic listening.[61]

Summary

- Listening constitutes a central part of organizational communication but is often not viewed as important as speaking and informing. There is a listening crisis in organizations.
- Strategic listening is a conscious, reflective, systematized, and goal-oriented listening process that makes organizations more responsive and agile to meet a complex reality better.
- Organizations should listen strategically to improve leadership, coworker leadership, and relationships with stakeholders such as customers and citizens.

Chapter 3

Listening Culture

IN A TRADITIONAL bureaucratic organizational hierarchy, managers are considered the most resourced and best suited to make wise decisions. In such a hierarchy, managers also have the highest status. As a result, those lower down in the organization are too often not seen as essential assets for the development and success of the organization. In other words, managers and leaders rarely listen to coworkers. In addition, many traditional organizations lack communication systems that support upward communication from coworkers with direct customer contact to senior management.

In the mid-1980s, the problems of the traditional bureaucratic organizational hierarchy were recognized. In the book *Moments of Truth*, Jan Carlzon states that the most outstanding values arise in the encounter between coworkers and customers.[1] For this reason, Carlzon argues that traditional organizational pyramids must be torn down and re-evaluated. Even in service management research, researchers have advocated for the inverted organizational pyramid since the late 1970s (Figure 3.1).

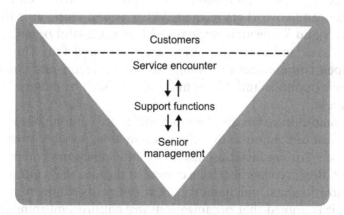

Figure 3.1 Service-oriented organizational structure.[2]

DOI: 10.4324/9781003413486-3

Coworkers who meet customers are seen as one of the most critical human resources since a large part of the value creation occurs in the meeting between coworkers and customers, users, or citizens. The organization should therefore ensure that it provides the conditions in terms of training, information, and powers to make decisions for coworkers as well as support from functions such as human resources (HR), finance, quality, and communication. There is then a more significant opportunity for strategic listening.

While it is crucial to review organizational structures, developing organizational culture is even more critical if strategic listening is to be realized. In this chapter, we will discuss organizational culture, the culture of silence, and how to create a culture of listening.

Organizational Culture

Organizational culture is about the commonalities in how people in a group or organization understand and value reality.[3] Another way of describing organizational culture is the norms, values, and perceptions of reality that coworkers and managers share.[4] These factors influence how events are perceived, problems are solved, and priorities are made.

In the 1980s, interest in and the importance of organizational culture became a high priority in organizations. Not least, the great success of Japanese companies on the world market was a driving force behind the interest in organizational culture. Many Western organizations tried to emulate this and worked to develop a so-called strong culture with given norms and values that could guide coworkers. The idea of building strong organizational cultures was to move from direct command leadership to values-based leadership, which means that leadership shifted to being inspirational, enthusiastic, and pointing out the direction and goals.

Two popular books that had a far-reaching impact were published in the 1980s—*In Search of Excellence*[5] by Tom Peters and Robert Waterman and *Corporate Cultures* by Terence E. Deal and Allan A. Kennedy.[6] These books provide advice on how organizations can develop a strong culture that can guide managers and coworkers in their decisions and work. It is interesting to note that Peters and Waterman emphasized that successful organizations listen to their coworkers and customers and dare to try and fail. This is only possible in an open communication climate where managers and coworkers dare to express their opinions and where mistakes are seen as material for learning and development.

Organizational culture has also been a popular area among researchers. Many have been critical of the notion that there is only one, possibly strong, culture in an organization.[7] An organization has many and sometimes competing cultures or subcultures. Research has also been critical of the idea that culture is a variable that an organization has, which management can easily shape, reshape and control.[8] Rather, it is argued that organizations *are* cultures, meaning that they are shaped and reshaped by the people working there, not something that managers can control. This latter understanding of organizational culture is claimed by many researchers to be the fundamental metaphor for how we should understand the culture in organizations.[9]

Organizational culture has re-emerged as an essential aspect of a successful organization. The importance of culture for cohesion and community in an organization and as a management tool was demonstrated during the Covid-19 pandemic. When coworkers worked from home, many felt disconnected from their organization. In most organizations, work tasks were being done well, but only some managers were engaging in communication to hold the organization together and strengthen the culture. As time passed, more and more routines were developed to meet digitally, perhaps for 15 minutes every day in the department, to see and hear each other, thus acknowledging each other as important people. Other organizations introduced pulse surveys and videoconferencing where management could inform and speak to coworkers but also take the opportunity to listen to them. The pandemic showed us how important it is to listen to each other and how influential culture is to an organization.[10]

New research suggests that in organizations where coworkers are allowed, willing, and able to speak up, managers are three to four times more likely to be active on internal social media platforms and carry through communication with coworkers.[11] In these organizational cultures, managers are much more likely to listen to coworkers and seek high levels of involvement as well as engagement among them. Research conducted by Cardon and his colleagues clearly shows that managers who operate in an organization with an open communication climate are more likely to use internal social media to communicate.[12] However, these managers are mainly focused on themselves, and this type of listening also tends to be asymmetrical. In other words, listening is not genuine and open, but is mainly about seeking confirmation of decisions already made. This research also suggests that in these organizations, efficiency is high. Coworkers do not expect symmetrical communication where both parties are genuinely interested in what the other has to say while prone to change their position. In addition, the researchers underscore that the coworkers included in the study—organizations in the United States—need to be used to genuine listening and having the opportunity to influence decisions.

Culture of Silence

A survey conducted by Novus Opinion on behalf of the Saco, the Swedish Confederation of Professional Associations, shows that 35 percent of coworkers at universities and colleges experience a culture of silence in their workplace.[16] Public organizations are reported on remarkably often, which can be explained by the fact that they are more open to journalists because of the principle of public access and coworkers' freedom of communication. The gaming company Paradox,[13] the European Criminal Police Office,[14] and the Police Authority[15] are examples of organizations where a culture of silence prevails, but there are many.

Now and then, articles appear in newspapers about the existence of cultures of silence in companies and public organizations. Often, coworkers blame their employer for a culture of silence, while managers deny this. What is true in this situation is difficult to determine, but the fact that coworkers *feel* that their voices are silenced and that they are not allowed to speak out is severe enough.

Hence, many examples of management silencing uncomfortable and problematic voices exist. Instead, input that supports the organization's original plans is valued more than those suggestions that challenge a change. Taken together, these barriers can lead to the development of a culture of silence, the increase of coworker self-censorship, and the silencing of voices. Regarding fewer career and development opportunities, there is simply too much at stake for a coworker to make their voice heard in the organization.

What Does a Culture of Silence Mean?

A culture of silence exists when coworkers and managers feel they must withhold potentially important information, mainly due to fear of punishments such as exclusion from the group or direct reprimands.[13] Silence in organizations is about more than just the absence of voices or opportunities to speak. Still, it is about *not* telling when you have a suggestion, a concern, information about a problem, or a dissenting opinion about something that you think is important.[14] The culture of silence is one of the main reasons why organizational change or development does not take place and why there needs to be more listening going on internally in organizations.[19] Moreover, the culture of silence is a demoralizing phenomenon. It leads to lower levels of engagement among coworkers and managers.[15]

Unfortunately, few managers realize how large a problem it is that coworkers are silent because of fear since it is not easily noticed.[16] When a person is silent and has something important to share, only that person knows what the others are missing. Unfortunately, some managers seem to believe, perhaps unconsciously, that fear motivates coworkers.[17] They seem to think that coworkers who are afraid of the consequences of underperforming will work harder and perform better. In practice, *management by fear* can sometimes work for simple tasks and repetitive jobs. Still, it will also lead to high staff turnover, more sick days, unmotivated coworkers, and lower productivity and quality. In highly skilled jobs requiring collaboration and continuous learning, fear is not a very good motivator. On the contrary, it is shown that fear effectively prevents learning and collaboration.

Why Do Cultures of Silence Emerge?

According to Morrison and Milliken, there are three main explanations for why cultures of silence emerge.[18] First, a culture of silence emerges when top management believes that coworkers are not interested in organization-wide issues, but rather are interested in themselves. This can lead management either to prevent upward communication implicitly or explicitly because managers think coworkers have no interest in supporting the organization's development.[19] Morrison and Milliken point out that these perceptions of coworkers are rarely conscious.

A second explanation, as already mentioned, is a strong assumption that management and managers are the ones who know best. There is also an assumption that managers must govern and control while coworkers should be non-questioning followers.[20] This can lead management and supervisors to engage only in quasi-dialogue and quasi-observation. However, managers are expected to engage in relationship-based or participative leadership in modern organizations. Through this form of leadership, listening is essential to shared decision-making and the organization's development. But in practice, it is just something that is said and not done; it is a veneer that is painted. Many managers follow the latest management trends—to look good on the surface. It becomes a form of window dressing without any real organizational change.[21] In the well-known bestseller *The Fifth Discipline*, the author Peter Senge writes that in many organizations, no learning takes place because they only engage in what the book calls *participatory openness*.[22] When participatory openness prevails, coworkers feel safe to express their views. There are also different opportunities and media platforms where people can make their voices heard. However, Senge points out that at a deeper level, no manager changes his or her mind, and no change takes place. Senge suggests that participatory openness is recognized by coworkers being able to say: "This was a good meeting—everyone got to say what they think", demonstrating the perception that if everyone gets to share their opinion, the problem is solved.

The opposite of participatory openness is *reflexive openness*. This starts with a willingness to challenge one's thinking and an understanding that any "certain understanding" of how reality works is, at best, only a hypothesis. There are always other ways of understanding reality, and there is always room to try out other ideas and solutions that can improve the organization's performance. In addition to a willingness to challenge one's assumptions, time must be set aside for reflection.

A third explanation for why a culture of silence may emerge relates to the common notion that consensus, agreement, and harmony are implications of a well-functioning organization. Too many managers assume that *no news is good news*, meaning that business is up and running and that things are rolling along perfectly fine.[23] On the other hand, disagreements and differences of opinion should be avoided at all costs. The consensus view contrasts with the pluralist alternative.[24] In a pluralist approach, disagreement is seen as usual and conflict as healthy. Even in research, there are notions that unity and finding common ground is the goal. Still, some researchers argue that it is through disagreement, dissent (i.e., constructive disagreement), and discussion that new knowledge can be developed.[25]

It is important to stress that it is not only managers who create and maintain a culture of silence. Coworkers also contribute to maintaining the silence culture and the silencing of other coworkers.[26] In every organization, there are one or more cultures, so-called subcultures, that have their dominant norms and values. If these are violated by someone, other coworkers are likely to point out or even punish the person who tries to break the preconceived established rules.

There is also a fourth explanation—*fear*—which is probably the most dominant explanation.[27] Fear is the strongest of human emotions and has contributed to the emergence of crises, the death of patients, the loss of market opportunities, the increase in sick leave, and so on. Coworkers have been afraid to make their voices heard and to deliver damaging information to managers and leadership. As a result, management has been unable to address a negative situation.

Eliminating a culture of silence is tricky but entirely possible. Morrison and Milliken emphasize that a prerequisite to this is that top management first becomes aware of why the culture of silence exists and then actively works to change the situation. This cannot be done over a coffee break, but requires long-term commitment and perseverance to bring about change.

How to Create a Listening Culture

Organizational culture significantly impacts how well listening functions within the organization.[28] An organizational culture that supports listening requires management to be committed and genuinely interested in listening to coworkers and customers. This, in turn, requires that coworkers and customers feel that they are being listened to and that management demonstrates that they are listening and consider the information they receive through listening. Gans and Zhan argue that there are reasons why coworkers in organizations do not make their voices heard, such as the strong narratives in many organizations that it is dangerous to criticize or talk about their own or others' mistakes.[29] This suggests that communicators in organizations need to start telling the narratives that managers and leaders care about coworkers' opinions and thoughts.

If there is no culture of listening in an organization, it is difficult to achieve effective strategic listening.[30] In a listening culture, coworkers feel *psychologically safe*; coworkers feel that there is an opportunity to voice dissent, criticize, and talk about mistakes without punishment.[31] Pery, Doytch, and Kluger highlight that:

When speakers feel heard, their psychological safety increases.[32]

If there is no psychological safety, there is a high risk of the emergence of a culture of silence. Psychological safety is also a concept mainly linked to the research of Amy C. Edmondson, a professor of business administration.[33] Edmondson has spent over 20 years researching teamwork and communication, among other things, and has found that psychological safety is the most critical *factor explaining organizational success* in private and public organizations. In an organization characterized by psychological safety, coworkers do not feel hindered or restricted by fear of embarrassment, ridicule, exclusion, threat, or other punishment for speaking up about their mistakes, failures, or dissenting views. Nor do they experience any fear of providing what may be perceived as negative information to the organization and its management. When psychological safety prevails, there is excellent potential for organizational learning, with managers and coworkers testing different solutions and thus occasionally making mistakes. These are seen here as material for learning—not as something that creates feelings of shame.

Another researcher who has studied psychological safety is William Kahn, a professor of management. In a study published in 1990, Kahn concluded that psychological safety creates coworker commitment.[34] When there is psychological safety in an organization, coworkers can engage and express themselves rather than disengage from the organization and spend energy defending themselves. Other research highlights the positive relationship between managers' ability to be humorous and coworkers' sense of psychological safety, which improves the conditions for coworkers to dare to speak up.[35]

Edmondson defines psychological safety as a climate where people feel comfortable expressing themselves and being themselves. This means that when psychological safety exists in an organization, managers and coworkers feel safe to share ongoing and perceived concerns and mistakes without fear of embarrassment or retaliation in the form of being shamed or ignored. A prerequisite for psychological safety is trust and respect between coworkers and managers. However, trust is not the same as psychological safety. Trust is about the interaction between individuals or parties and exists in people's minds.

It is defined as follows: "trust is a psychological state that arises from a willingness to accept vulnerability and risk-taking based on positive expectations of the intentions and actions of others".[36] Psychological safety is experienced at the group level when individuals working together have a similar perception of whether psychological safety exists in the organization. Annika Telléus, the author of the book *Konsten att lyssna* (*Eng.* The Art of Listening), says that the first step towards psychological safety in an organization is for coworkers in a group or department to start discussing how they want to be listened to and what each person can do to make it easier for each other to be heard.[37]

The literature on trust-based leadership emphasizes that trust is suitable for organizations for various reasons. However, in the book *Openness and the Trust Spiral*, which does not discuss trust-based leadership but trust more generally, Anders Wendelheim and Kerstin Rodell Lundgren provide much concrete advice on how trust and openness can be developed in an organization.[38] They point out that trust is something that is earned. In other words, it is impossible to command or demand that coworkers feel trust and show openness. Of course, working actively to achieve greater trust and openness in an organization is possible. But it is a process of change that requires much work and will take time. Nevertheless, the more traditional management literature gives the impression that this is a simple matter. But transparency is not for cowards! It takes a lot of courage and personal maturity to dare to open up to others. And it is challenging in a professional context where the power aspect is constantly present and influences relationships. Wendelheim and Rodell Lundgren note that:

> *An openness that leads to trust is not a cure-all for cowards or a Band-Aid that cures everything or fixes a problem. It takes much courage, especially if there are tough and complex decisions to be made, to dare to confront someone, approach a necessary conflict, and say what needs to be said.*[39]

Management and managers are role models for other coworkers in the organization. The success of a trusting climate depends on the actions of managers. Managers must demonstrate the courage to be assertive and clear while remaining vulnerable. So, for a culture of listening to emerge where coworkers feel psychologically safe, trust and openness are needed.

Wendelheim and Rodell argue that there is a reciprocal relationship between openness and trust. If there is no openness, there is no trust. And vice versa: if there is no trust, there is no openness. However, Wendelheim and Rodell point out an essential difference between openness and trust. One's openness can be controlled and managed, while trust describes an earned relationship between people. In other words, trust results from how people act toward other people. Being open in a professional context is about telling each other how you perceive each other's behavior and not about how you are as a private person. Wendelheim and Rodell underline that trust requires a person to be willing to be vulnerable, to dare to speak up and say how they perceive things, and to dare to take the necessary conflicts.

Brené Brown has been researching vulnerability and courage for over 20 years. In her book, *Daring Greatly*, Brown defines vulnerability as uncertainty, risk-taking, and emotional nakedness.[40] Brown writes that honest, constructive, and engaging criticism characterizes courageous organizational cultures. In a courageous organizational culture, there is much feedback between managers and coworkers and between coworkers. All people need to receive feedback and feel appreciated as individuals. Increased organizational feedback also increases opportunities for learning, critical thinking, and change. However, as Brown points out, we must be aware that this creates discomfort when we are asked to develop and learn new things. Here senior management and managers must point out that it is normal to feel anxiety, shame, and fear when we receive feedback and try to learn new things.

Thus, individuals can start a positive spiral where increased openness leads to increased trust (see Figure 3.2). This, in turn, creates the conditions for more openness, leading to further increased trust between individuals. So, in many ways, it is up to individuals to challenge the group and be more open than trust allows. When such courage is shown, the group evolves. Psychologists tend to argue that personal development occurs when one experiences something unpleasant, recalcitrant, or unusual and nevertheless carries out an action.

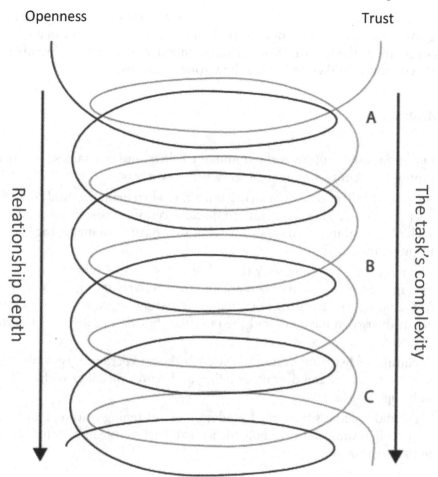

Openness   Trust

Relationship depth

The task's complexity

A

B

C

Figure 3.2 Openness and the spiral of trust.[41]

While everyone has a shared responsibility to develop openness and trust in a group or organization, managers and the leadership team have a particular responsibility to act as role models for others. If senior managers set an example, other managers will likely follow suit. One manager we believe to be a role model for many other managers is the former director general of the Swedish Transport Administration, Lena Eriksson. When she started as the senior manager in 2015, Lena began by traveling around to the various locations in Sweden where the agency operates. These trips aimed to strengthen the relationship with the coworkers and increase her trust. Since she started at the Swedish Transport Administration, relationship building has been critical to her. According to Lena Eriksson, you should not underestimate the importance of movement within and across departments in an organization by grabbing a coffee and talking with new coworkers. This reduces the distance to management and builds trust within the organization. Showing courage is also one of Eriksson's cornerstones of successful leadership, and she urges managers and coworkers to be open and honest about what they think. Eriksson says, "Sure, I make mistakes. And I think wrong. And it gets . . . you're not a superhuman person".[42] Trust can be built by being open about the fact that you are only human, that you are vulnerable, and at times commit mistakes and make the wrong decisions.

Summary

- Organizational culture is the dominant beliefs, norms, values, and perceptions of reality among managers and coworkers.
- A culture of silence exists in an organization when managers and coworkers perceive that they are afraid to disclose certain types of information, such as critical information or mistakes that have been made, for fear of being punished.
- The main way to counteract the culture of silence is by making senior management aware of its existence and then actively trying to counteract it, including by acting as role models and showing courage by talking about their own mistakes and the fact that they do not always have the answers.
- A culture of listening occurs when coworkers experience psychological safety—that they can dissent, criticize, and report mistakes without fear of being punished.
- Trust and openness form the foundation of a listening culture; managers have a big responsibility to take the lead and act as role models for others in the organization.

Chapter 4

How to Become a Better Listener

WE ALL LIKE and appreciate persons who are good at listening. A good listener is perceived as a better communicator, and as they are more likely to be admired, they are perceived as more trustworthy.[1] This is an important reason for all of us to strive to become better at listening. More people will treasure our company, and a good listener will be better positioned than others to build trusting relationships. Not least, persons who develop their listening skills will be better parents, partners, family members, and friends. If we become better at listening to those we have a relationship with, the relationship is reinforced because we feel seen and validated. But at the same time, we all know that listening is difficult.

We read the following observation on LinkedIn:

Before you answer; Listen
Before you go on the defensive; Listen
Before you start thinking; Listen
Before you start finding solutions; Listen
Before you start talking about your experience; Listen.
Listening at work and at home.
We are too bad at listening!
So, listen.[2]

This post and exhortation summarize what we should all be doing to become better listeners. We should stop and reflect on whether we, in different situations, are really listening or are mainly focusing on ourselves. Of course, this is not easy. Listening to someone else should be the easiest thing in the world. We learned to listen before we started talking. We all have done it and do it all the time in our daily lives, privately and professionally. Yet we know that this is not always easy in practice, and the autopilot quickly kicks in when we go about our business as usual. We interrupt and respond before we have finished listening and let our minds wander elsewhere. We lose concentration on the other person or focus on ourselves too much and start thinking about what we feel,

DOI: 10.4324/9781003413486-4

what we think, or what we should say to the other person. It is easy to interrupt and say something like: "That made me think of that time when I . . .", "No, I don't agree with you there—that's not how it is", or "But you don't have to feel that way".

We often defend ourselves when we feel threatened or attacked before we have finished listening. Or we try to formulate solutions to help the other person without the other person asking for a solution. The other person may want us to listen to them, to think out loud, to air their thoughts, or to just be validated. However, this very human way of acting does nothing positive for our ability to listen, neither in our professional practice nor our private life.

But why do we humans act this way? Why is it so hard to listen, although listening to others makes us wiser and contributes to us constantly evolving and learning as human beings? To avoid taking a "mental holiday" when we listen, we must learn to become better and wiser as listeners:

Good listeners use the time to analyze or reconsider the information they receive. But most untrained listeners use the time to take a mental holiday.[3]

In this chapter, we will focus on practical ways to become a better listener.

The Right Attitude: A Prerequisite

We emphasized in previous chapters that communication is about *speaking and listening*. Yet too often, we—individuals and organizations—focus on information dissemination or speaking when communicating. Too often, we have overconfidence that the information will lead us to a new understanding, new knowledge, changed behavior, or whatever the goal of our communication may be. One explanation for why we spend so much time, and energy, disseminating information is probably because it is perceived as the easier way out. It also feels relieving to show that we have accomplished something, while it takes longer to devote time to listening and seeing an impact. The manager who has sent a message can show that she has communicated with her coworkers and acted. Thus, despite the many positive effects of listening, we spend too much time in our daily lives communicating verbally rather than engaging in dialogue and listening. It has been said before, but it bears repeating.

Psychology researcher Carl R. Rogers and leadership researcher Fritz J. Roethlisberger argue in a classic article from 1952 that excellent communication always starts with the individual and that listening is necessary for organizations to be effective.[4] We can communicate more freely and effectively with others when we understand ourselves better. They also stress that proper communication takes place when we listen with understanding. This means that we try to understand an idea or attitude from the other person's perspective and how it is experienced by the other person. But oftentimes, it is like this:

Most people do not listen with the intention to understand; they listen with the intention to respond.[5]

As we mentioned before, listening is often more difficult and complex than we believe. However, it is important to remember that listening is an ability, not a personality trait. In other words, listening is an ability that can be trained and can therefore be compared to a muscle. It requires practice, perseverance, effort, and willingness to become a better listener. However, real listening also requires a specific type of approach. In the box that follows, the well-known management consultant Tom Peters provides his understanding of listening:

> **Tom Peter's Thoughts on Listening**[6]
>
> Listening is NOT a skill—you can learn a few techniques, but this is not genuine listening. Listening is, above all, an attitude. If you are uninterested in the person, your body language will show it. This is also why so many senior people are not good at listening—their attitude (I'm more brilliant, more successful, more important, need to answer this question, know the way forward, etc.) gets in the way. Your interest in the other person must be genuine. Your head must be empty of your thoughts—you must be one with another person.
>
> When preparing for a meeting (e.g., a coaching meeting with a coworker or a 1:1 with a client), most people prepare notes, things to discuss, etc.—but how many prepare their mindset and consciously empty their minds?
>
> Be curious!

Tom Peter's advice is to be more interested in the person we are listening to and not depart from our own beliefs, thoughts, or feelings. Trying to be more interested in others without judgment is the key to genuine listening. So, the basis for becoming a good listener does not in itself require any specific behavior; first and foremost, it is about adopting a particular attitude where one is open to the perceptions, knowledge, and experiences of others.[7] The willingness and intention to listen is the *key to good listening*. This is confirmed by a significant psychological research study by Avraham N. Kluger and Guy Itzchakov, who published the study in a highly acclaimed article, "The Power of Listening at Work".[8] Good listening requires a willingness to see reality through the eyes of others without judging or evaluating based on one's own beliefs. If a listener succeeds in doing this, he or she has come a long way.

Train Your Listening Skills

In addition to having the right attitude when listening, you can improve your listening ability through personal development and training. There is no ready-made model or method for assessing individuals' listening skills.[9] Nor is there any research showing that those perceived to be effective listeners are better listeners than others.[10] The existing methods focus very much on visible indicators, such as the listener asking questions or acknowledging the other person. Brownell argues that those who train managers and coworkers to become better listeners must develop courses with clearly defined learning outcomes and evaluation measures.[11] Still, listening is primarily a process that is difficult or even impossible to observe and, therefore, not easy to measure. Measurement also becomes problematic when people have different needs, experiences, expectations, and understanding of listening. Apparently, one person may perceive a manager as a good listener, while another may have a completely different idea of what constitutes good listening. This must also be considered when working with strategic listening—everyone has different understandings and expectations of what good listening means. In conclusion, although measuring people's listening skills is difficult or even impossible, this does not imply that we in organizations should not develop and practice these skills. There is already much research showing the great benefits of being a good listener.

Let Emotions Be a Support and Not a Hindrance!

We all have emotions, yet too many persons do not understand their value and importance. A significant part of the idea of going to therapy is to understand better how strongly our emotions affect us. Our emotions have helped us humans to be successful throughout history. However, emotions are also a great hindrance to us, and in many contexts, our emotions can make it difficult or even impossible for us to act. We all react with emotions to what happens, what we think might happen, or what the English philosopher John Shotter calls *"the unsaid"*—unspoken assumptions and interpretations about what is meant.[12] Researchers have begun to take an interest in the role of emotions in professional organizational contexts. It is therefore vital that we take emotions seriously and that we learn to relate to them. It is also essential to reflect on what we are emotionally reacting to:

Have self-compassion—you can't scream at your own brain like a sergeant and whip that brain into shape. What you can do is recognize your weaknesses and make the necessary adjustments.[13]

Learn from Priests: Experts in Listening

Some professionals are particularly good at listening, for example, police officers, psychologists, doctors, social workers, and priests. Listening to people in grief and crisis is part of the professional role of a priest, and this part of the priesthood is called pastoral care. Following this topic, we interviewed Bo Johansson, a priest and former pastor.

Bo Johansson believes that listening is an essential aspect of our society to bring individuals together and form communities. "We are there for each other—no man is an island. And alone is not strong! We need each other, and we are always stronger together". Johansson points out that people's identity emerges and is created when the self meets the other. When we listen to others, we can grow as people and become wiser, which is also true in organizations. If we, as coworkers and managers, listen more to each other, we establish suitable conditions for development, innovation, and learning.

Bo Johansson points out that in many everyday situations, listening is not realized at all. An example is what can happen during a dinner party when most people are not particularly interested in listening to others but mainly want to tell their own stories. When we hear other people talk, most of us immediately associate what they say with what we have experienced. One thing that Bo Johansson was taught at the seminary was that when you listen, you should never say to the person telling you, "I understand exactly how you feel. I feel the same way myself". The person telling the story will immediately feel that the listener is focusing on himself or herself, which is unsuitable for active listening. In the worst-case scenario, the speaker stops opening up and sharing their thoughts and opinions.

We asked Bo Johansson the question of how we can become better listeners. He reflected that in the role of a pastor, or when you want to engage in listening, the most important thing is to try to step out of your ego and step into the other person's life for a moment. This is a challenge for most of us, and we need to practice this repeatedly. Johansson stresses, "Taking the other person's perspective is tricky. It's a high threshold. And you must then not start telling people about yourself but listen to what the other person says". One way to help in this is to realize that everyone has the same value, a prerequisite for listening to anyone, even those who arouse antipathy in us.

When we listen, we are influenced by the speaker, and we can feel sympathy or antipathy. According to Bo Johansson, what is crucial for us when we listen to others is that we perceive that what is being told is honest. In other words, the person telling the story is transparent and fair, not trying to convey a picture that does not correspond to reality. When we believe that the person we are listening to is honest, we will continue to listen and gain energy from listening.

In the box that follows, we have listed some advice from Bo Johansson on creating the best listening conditions.

How to Create the Conditions for Good Listening

- Be in a closed room to exclude disturbing impressions and sounds.
- Use the time as a game piece and a resource—make sure you set aside plenty of time for listening. If the other person perceives a lack of time, she will probably stop speaking and turn quiet.
- Physical presence enhances the possibilities for good listening in comparison to digital meetings.

Ask Questions!

A good listener *truly cares about* understanding what is being said and is better at asking questions to understand the speaker's meaning.[14] There is a surprising power in asking questions that, in many organizations and for many individuals, is an overutilized resource.[15] Indeed, questions are a powerful tool for creating value within an organization. It stimulates learning and the exchange of ideas between colleagues, managers, and other stakeholders. In addition, questions inspire innovation and outstanding performance within the organization. Asking questions builds trust and shows interest in another person being acknowledged as necessary. People's emotional intelligence increases when we ask questions, which leads to learning and improving our capability to formulate questions. By asking questions, we create value for the organization and those we ask questions of—an excellent example of how value can be co-created.

The problem is that we generally spend too little time asking questions; when we do, we do not optimally do this. It is common for people to complain that others *ask too few* questions. For example, we are recalling the dinner party when we sat next to someone and were not asked a single question the entire evening. Meanwhile, since we are curious individuals, we ask many questions. While the neighbor next to us at the dinner table became increasingly excited, the evening experience suffered from the one-way communication of us asking all the questions without receiving any. Questions are a way of validating another person, and it is often a good feeling to be confirmed. Unfortunately, it can drain the energy of the person who takes responsibility for asking questions and never receives any questions in return. Of course, the other person, the questioner, also wants to talk about himself or herself and their thoughts on various issues.

Why is it like this? There are many reasons. As we have mentioned several times, our ego gets in the way of good listening. We do not think about asking questions of the other person, as we are so full of ourselves. There may be indifference, simply not caring, believing oneself bored by the answers, or being overconfident in one's knowledge and thinking that one already knows the answer. But there may also be reasons, such as a concern about asking the wrong questions and being perceived as rude or ignorant. However, the most common reason is that people do not comprehend the value of asking good questions.

To become better at asking questions, you also need to have a genuine interest in others and their perspectives and start practicing asking more questions. But which questions to ask and when? It depends, of course, on the situation and the objectives of the conversation. Here are a few:

- *Open questions* are better than yes and no questions. Open questions provide more information and increase opportunities to learn new things. For instance, if you are to ask someone if they enjoy their work, do not just ask, "Do you enjoy work?" but rather, "What do you think is good about your job and what do you think could be improved?" Open questions often start with "why" or "how". Of course, open questions are not appropriate in all contexts, for example, when you are in a negotiation and do not want to reveal information to the other party.

- *Follow-up questions* are often good because they signal that you are listening, are interested, and want to know more. This helps the respondent to feel acknowledged and listened to. An excellent follow-up question that hopefully deepens our understanding is: "Why?" A well-known Swedish sociologist, Johan Asplund, says more boldly, "Why the hell is that so?"[16] Asplund argues that we easily fall into "aspect blindness", where we fail to see what is outside the given. Therefore, we should constantly strive to find alternative explanations that provide greater understanding.

- *Sensitive questions* that may be perceived as intrusive should not be asked at the beginning of a conversation if you want to establish a relationship with your interlocutor.[17] It is important to start easy, with less sensitive questions, and then increase sensitivity as the conversation continues. Gradually, people will become more open and informative in their responses. The opposite may be true in other situations, where the most challenging questions may come first. People then tend to open up early in the conversation. Although socially it may seem odd, various studies have shown that this is how it works.

- *Open-up questions* acknowledge the fact that group dynamics play a role in asking questions. Someone in a group must take responsibility for open-up questions when groups meet. If no one opens up within the group, not much information is likely to be shared. However, if someone shares their thoughts more openly, it is easier for others in the group to follow suit.

Finally, questions and thoughtful responses create opportunities for smoother and more effective interactions, strengthening mutual understanding and trust, which can lead individuals and groups to discoveries.

Sometimes we talk to control people or situations. Sometimes we speak so that we don't have to listen to ourselves. Either way, when we talk to another person, our whole system becomes more tense. When we listen, we are more relaxed.[18]

Summary: How to Become a Better Listener

- Have the willingness to listen and take an interest in the other person. This is the first step on the road to becoming an effective listener. You must decide to become a better listener. As we have discussed in this chapter, it is primarily a matter of having the right attitude and wanting to listen to what others have to say.

- Give your full attention to the person you are listening to by looking at the person while not doing other things simultaneously. Try to interpret their body language and do not let your mind wander or let yourself speculate about what the person will say or start to think about what you will say yourself.
- Do not interrupt; let the speaker finish before you talk. Encourage the other person to continue talking and ask them to clarify if you do not understand.
- Acknowledge the other person's feelings, for example, by stating, "I understand it must have been difficult". It is essential to try to focus on the human aspect and that we humans need to feel validated and listened to.
- Do not judge the other person based on your own beliefs or interests. When the speaker feels that he or she is not being judged, he or she will feel free to tell the story without trying to make an impression.[19] He or she will also feel psychologically safe.

Chapter 5

Listening Leadership

MANAGERS AND OTHERS in leadership positions in organizations play major roles in strategic listening. They act as role models, and if they listen, it is more likely that other coworkers in the organization will follow their example and listen. Accordingly, there is a clear connection between good leadership and good listening.[1] When we perceive that we are being listened to, we happily let us be led by the other and also attribute leadership qualities to these individuals in a natural and unforced way. This chapter discusses the connection between listening and leadership and offers advice on how managers can become better listeners. Furthermore, it is possible to become better at listening by practicing it:

I wish I could find an institute that teaches people how to listen. After all, a good manager needs to listen at least as much as he [sic] needs to talk. Too many people fail to realize that good communication goes in both directions.[2]

Traditional Managers Do Not Listen

For a long time, the main task for managers has been to inform and instruct and, to some extent, direct and control coworkers. Moreover, research suggests that managers tend to get stuck in these patterns of verbally informing and instructing coworkers.[3] In one study, Elvnäs shows that managers spend 90 percent of their working hours talking, even though instructing and informing often have little effect. Although society has undergone significant changes, many organizations and managers insist on leading, organizing, and managing their activities according to old principles. Even if research since the mid-1990s has emphasized that managers should act as coaches and support coworkers, little has changed in practice. The same goes for listening, which unfortunately occurs too seldom or is not genuine. Writing in the *Harvard Business Review*, management consultant

DOI: 10.4324/9781003413486-5

Ram Charan states that one in four managers has a *listening deficit*, which can lead to many negative consequences.[4] If the CEO resists listening, the company may lose its foothold in the market and even disappear. There are obvious risks to this listening deficit, and we conclude that managers should listen more than they speak; listening leadership is crucial to a company's success and survival.

For the individual manager, it can be challenging to fulfill leadership expectations. In both research and popular literature, idealized images of a manager as a hero circulate—a strong and almost superhuman being expected to have all the answers and know best.[5] Managers are also described in this literature as having strong opinions and attitudes.[6] The understanding of a manager as the lone hero appears everywhere in society—in conversations, books, magazines, and even in Hollywood movies. The result, unfortunately, is that managers miss the fact that coworkers are essential knowledge resources, often experts in their fields, and well worth listening to.

The glorification of leadership in academia and popular literature can be demonstrated by the following quote from the American executive Kevin Sharer, a senior executive at General Electric. Sharer explains how he used to work:

My approach was: "I'm the smartest guy in the room. Just let me prove that here, in the first five minutes". I would even interrupt people and tell them what they were going to tell me, to save time so that we could get to the really important stuff, which was me telling them what to do. And I got away with it. It worked. Until it didn't.[7]

Sharer warns other managers that it is easy to fall into what he calls the *ego danger zone*—the risk of egocentricity where the spotlight is always focused on the manager as a person. Bryant and Sharer advise managers that it can be a good idea to stop and think about the acronym WAIT: "Why Am I Talking".[8] It is suitable for a person to reflect on whether they need to say what they are about to say. Instead, perhaps the best thing to do in this specific situation is to be quiet and devote time to listening.

Why Do Managers Not Listen?

In the introduction to this book, we addressed Jim Macnamara's assertion that there is a listening crisis both in organizations and in society.[9] Part of this crisis can be explained by managers' difficulty and sometimes inability to listen, maybe because they do not see it as essential and therefore do not focus on listening in their daily work. The failure of managers to listen is severe, as it hampers the ability of individuals and groups to act.[10]

In more traditional leadership research, the manager is portrayed as a hero who is solitary, strong, knowledgeable, decisive, risk-taking, charismatic, and in control.[11] This narrative, or a kind of mythmaking, persists today, but it neither fosters nor creates the conditions for listening. It is not entirely true that it is just a myth, as many managers in today's organizations also try to live up to this ideal. However, few associate well-functioning listening with the lone, strong, and decisive manager.

There are, of course, further explanations for why managers do not listen. The section that follows presents some of these explanations:

- *Listening is viewed as a passive activity, almost a non-activity.* Managers describe feeling more effective when they talk and make decisions based on the information they already have. Managers, therefore, do not value listening exceptionally highly. Instead, dissemination of information, output in various media, visibility, and image are valued more than listening and dialogue.[12]

- *Listening is not viewed as a career factor* because it is not valued as an essential skill and activity by senior management.[13] Instead, managers' one-way communication is rewarded, as if the manager is the one who speaks and provides the answers on how to solve problems. Speaking becomes an apparent factor for success and is rewarded career-wise. In the book *Becoming a Manager* by Linda Hill, several young managers who have been promoted to more managerial responsibilities are interviewed about what they find problematic in their new role.[14] As new managers, they find that coworkers demand that they listen more to them. This creates a sense of uncertainty. The managers interviewed describe that they are more comfortable providing information, making decisions, and suggesting solutions to problems. The career factor for these managers has decisively been their ability to speak convincingly and not to listen.

- *Managers who listen to risk are perceived as weak.*[15] Unfortunately, listening is too often associated with weakness—at least compared to speaking, which is considered an expression of power. The fact that listening is seen as an expression of weakness may have to do with the fact that it has historically been understood and equated with subordination and obedience.[16] Perhaps this understanding has accompanied listening as a concept and activity into the 21st century. Listening is seen as or gives a sense of losing power and control, hence a loss of status. However, it is essential to point out that research shows that managers who practice active listening gain status and prestige rather than being perceived as weak.[17] The excessively talkative manager may be perceived as dominant and slightly intimidating instead.

- *Listening can be perceived as time- and energy-consuming.*[18] This is partly true, as it is an investment in time and energy. But time can also be saved by listening and asking questions to coworkers. Information and instructions to coworkers become much more evident when the manager engages in the dialogue. Having frequent dialogues with coworkers and asking questions rather than distributing information often lead to greater clarity. Managers then need to spend less time explaining and answering questions, and coworkers, in turn, do not need to ask questions.[19]

- *Listening may entail that the manager needs to reconsider or change his or her mind.* When the manager listens more, without evaluating and judging what is said, instead of talking, he or she enters the perspective of others. This may challenge one's perspective and "force" one to realize that there may be other ways of understanding the world. Managers tend to enclose themselves in their information bubble and seem more inclined to surround themselves with yes-men. This shields them from skepticism but also prevents them from rethinking their worldviews.[20] Listening provides new insights about coworkers, which, in turn, may lead to the manager needing to change his or her position and attitude or modify decisions already made. This may be perceived as a loss of prestige, especially if the manager has loudly informed all coworkers of his or her position. It becomes easier not to change one's mind but to do what was intended, a phenomenon that can be understood as a form of *mental laziness.*[21]

By pointing out some of the significant challenges of leadership and listening, new possibilities for developing an organization arise. It is only when the problems become visible that they can be solved. Management researchers Marilyn M. Helms and Paula J. Haynes argue that this is important because:

> *[I]t has been found that effective managers spend more time actively seeking information from coworkers than talking.*[22]

Listening: An Overlooked Leadership Tool

Both in sources found online and in books, there are plenty of quotes from famous business leaders and politicians about the importance of listening in organizations. Richard Branson, the owner of Virgin Records and Virgin Atlantic, states the following on the importance of listening:

> *If you want to become a great leader, it is more important to be a good listener than a good speaker, because nobody learns anything by hearing themselves speak.*[23]

Listening implies a change in the approach to leadership, where the focus is not on the manager and his or her delivery or performance.[24] Training courses and literature suggest that managers should no longer derive from themselves but take a greater interest in their coworkers. Instead of telling coworkers what to do, modern managers ask open-ended questions and consider their views when making decisions.[25] One person who constantly in his career pointed out the importance of asking questions is Peter Drucker, considered to be the founding father of modern leadership research. As early as 1955, he stated in his book *The Practice of Management* that the critical and challenging job for managers is never to give the correct answers—it is to find the right questions.[26]

The emerging modern leadership does not put the manager at the center, but understands leadership as a process exercised by both managers and coworkers. Managers and coworkers drive leadership together, even if the manager has ultimate responsibility. Emerging leadership, which in some research is said to be agile, requires goals and decisions to change as conditions change. Here, coworkers are seen as essential resources with excellent skills and knowledge that are important for making decisions. Viewing coworkers as wise and knowledgeable creates better conditions for making successful decisions. Hence, listening skills are critical for effective management communication.[27]

Furthermore, in the book *See the Human! My Story of Success, Difficult People and the Art of Listening*, Jan Carlzon concludes that managers need to listen more to their coworkers and gives the following advice:

If you want to bring people along, you need to make them feel something. You must create a feeling in the recipient and not just deliver information.[28]

Instead of giving speeches and distributing information, managers should ask questions and provide feedback. If the manager does not know what the coworkers need, they can ask them.[29]

Managers who listen and ask questions gain many benefits, such as increased trust, job satisfaction, and team spirit. They help coworkers to be relaxed, aware of their strengths and weaknesses, and inclined to reflect on themselves without being so intent on being on the defense. This, in turn, supports coworkers to be more open-minded to others' opinions and more willing to cooperate with coworkers.

Managers are essential role models for coworkers in the organization. Managers who encourage others to listen set an example and reward behavior that comprises listening. Over time, this creates positive environments for listening, which many studies confirm has a positive impact on an organization's financial performance.[30] *Listening is simply an overlooked leadership tool.*[31]

The need to be listened to also increases in crises, as mentioned earlier in the section on organizational culture. Research on leadership in crises, such as the Covid-19 pandemic, shows that coworkers' need for leaders to support, care, and acknowledge has increased.[32] Managers can provide these social and human needs to coworkers by listening, providing feedback, and ensuring they are present in the organization. Further research on leadership during the Covid-19 pandemic shows that the great uncertainty, ambiguity, and complexity that arose also increased the need for managers who are good at listening.[33]

What Is Needed of Managers to Become Better Listeners?

Managers have a significant part in and bear extensive responsibilities for listening during crises. At the same time, we know that many managers need new insights, education, and training to become better listeners.[34] In many management programs and courses taught at business schools, presentation *skills* are commonly included and are a priority in the learning outcomes. However, only a few courses provide anything related to listening. We believe this is a pity since good leadership is strongly linked to good listening. Tom Peters explains:

Excellence is to shut up and listen—really listen/aggressively listen.[35]

Decide to Become a Good Listener

The first step to becoming a better listener is to decide that you want to develop your skills: "I want to become a better listener!" This decision needs to be at the top of your action list. Given the explanations for the listening deficit we mentioned at the outset, making this decision is unlikely to be easy and requires a special effort!

Managers who want to become better listeners will undoubtedly find it difficult to live up to this decision if they do not notice some positive effects quite rapidly. Some advice for any manager whenever one feels tempted to interrupt or hinder a coworker who is talking is to let them know that you are now only devoting yourself to listening for a few minutes.[36] This will break the old pattern and allow time for reflection on what is being said. It also allows the coworker to think out loud and test their thoughts on someone genuinely listening.

It is essential to acknowledge that listening can be challenging and that efforts to listen genuinely can result in failed outcomes now and then. It is therefore important to convince yourself that failure is okay and a natural part of human development. Grint underlines that managers find it worse to admit a mistake than to continue on the chosen path, even if it turns out to be wrong.[37] Because there is such a widespread perception of traditional leadership, one must first become aware of it and then try to break this outdated perception. If you do so, you will gradually develop a listening attitude that will make it easier to listen to your coworkers without wanting to defend yourself and interrupt the other person.

Listening Requires Effort

Listening requires far more effort and training than managers oftentimes realize.[38] It is partly about investing time to gain new insights and to practice doing one's job in new ways. These efforts will pay off, as they will bring comfort to the managerial job. Listening will also make a person a better speaker.[39] As a result, the information and instructions managers give through speaking become much more straightforward.[40] This increases coworkers' autonomy because they do not have to come back and ask clarifying questions to their managers. So, if managers can be prepared to contribute with some effort, it will also contribute to various gains in the managerial role. There is also an over-belief that clarity and being in a dialogue take more time than doing the talking and being in a monologue alone. However, this is short-term thinking. In the long run, it is always better to involve coworkers and customers in dialogue and to listen to them carefully.

One crucial insight is that leadership is not about what managers do, but what the managers get others to do.[41] To succeed, managers need to make an apparent effort and start taking an interest in their coworkers. A good start is to listen to coworkers' needs to understand how they perceive and experience things.

Advice from a Leadership Coach: Annelie Brzezinska

The starting point for being a good listener is to be interested in listening. Without interest, one cannot listen. When listening, you need to be able to tune out the noise. Both inner noise as well as an external noise.

You need to listen actively with your entire body, and your body needs to signal that you are listening. You should open your heart, turn off your brain for a little while, and try to listen without preconceptions. Do not prejudge, which can be very easy to do. Do not sit and think of your answers as you listen. Your task is to make the speaker become and feel like their best self.

You Could Be Wrong

One insight that Simon Elvnäs points out in his book *Effective* is to assume that you can be wrong and that others can be right.[42] Björn Natthiko Lindeblad writes similarly in his book *I May Be Wrong and Other Wisdoms from Life as a Forest Monk*.[43] Jan Carlzon draws the same conclusions: "Whenever I spoke, I derived from myself. I was very much like, 'I think, I believe, I decide'. People around me reacted and thought I had become egocentric without even noticing".[44] This realization can be challenging because, as we mentioned earlier, it can lead one to reconsider decisions or change his or her mind.

It is common for managers to believe they have been appointed managers because they know and understand more than anyone else—deriving solely from themselves and viewing themselves as a prerequisite for others to be able to do their job. However, the most important thing is that coworkers understand, can, and know what to do. This is why managers must ensure coworkers know what to do and what is expected. The easiest way to discover this is by asking questions and listening to the answers. Unfortunately, too many managers overestimate their knowledge and think they are always right while underestimating the power of asking questions to coworkers. Asking questions increases the chances of developing the insight that one may be wrong—an insight that may be very valuable. Nobel laureate Daniel Kahneman reflects:

Being wrong is the only way I feel sure I've learned anything.[45]

Courage to Show Yourself Vulnerable

Becoming a good listener requires the courage to show yourself vulnerable.[46] This, in turn, requires a certain amount of personal development, maturity, and confidence. Often, managers do not listen because they want to *appear to* have the situation under control, a control they feel that they maintain by speaking. However, this is not a successful path, especially in a society that is becoming increasingly complex and hence difficult to understand and control. Psychologists Robert Kegan and Lisa Lahey argue that we all focus too much on hiding weaknesses and vulnerabilities[47] in an attempt to cultivate the image of ourselves as strong and decisive managers.

In the book *The Gifts of Imperfection*, sociologist Brené Brown challenges traditional notions of perfectionism, the expectations that we always need to be perfect, and that we only want to hear about success and things that are going well.[48] In Western societies, many people are driven by perfectionism. Brown writes that shame loves perfectionists and oftentimes silences them. This is because we are afraid to disappoint others or be alienated when discussing times when we were not perfect. Brown stresses that shame is a general human fear of not being liked or ostracized from the group. However, we know that life is complex, and people's lives are not merely about feeling good or being happy. Brown says that one way to break free from this limiting mindset is by strengthening shame tolerance. *Shame tolerance* is a person's ability to recognize shame, deal with it, and get through it constructively, thereby developing better courage, self-esteem, and a sense of community. One of the best ways to deal with shame is to talk about your feelings and articulate how you feel. So, talk to a good friend or a therapist. Talking about and identifying your feelings of shame will allow you to distance yourself from the problem and manage your intense feelings. It can also be helpful to distinguish between feelings of shame and feelings of guilt. Whereas shame is about who we are as persons and our identities, guilt is about how we behave. So, whenever shame arises, you experience: "Something is wrong with me". However, when guilt arises, you feel: "I did wrong".

Reflect on Your Behavior

It is common for people to believe that they are performing better than they are. Both managers and coworkers often perceive their performance as higher than that of others. Similarly, research suggests that managers do not devote as much time to tasks as they think they do. This is because they think they are listening, asking questions, and giving feedback. However, studies have shown that managers are primarily engaged in talking. While managers state they spend 40 percent of their time providing feedback, this is rarely more than 5 percent in practice. In addition, measurements of the general nature of coworker-manager conversations show that 60 to 80 percent is spent talking about how things are.

Consequently, managers think they are coaching and giving feedback, but as mentioned earlier, they give their coworkers information and instructions. Simon Elvnäs proposes that managers need to become more aware, learning to do what they think they are doing—and intend to do.[49] Leadership researcher Stefan Söderfjäll points out that acting often requires taking a back seat to talk about action.[50] Talk becomes a substitute for action, and it becomes more comfortable to talk about doing than to do. Talking about values, strategies, openness, and perhaps the value of listening creates a sense of having acted through one's talk. However, changing habits and behaviors takes practice. It is therefore time to reduce the time spent talking and start listening.

How to Make Managers Better Listeners!

A scientific article on leadership and listening published in the *International Journal of Listening* 2022 underlines the importance of organizations developing managers' listening skills by introducing it as a component of internal training programs. The same article stresses that the ability to listen should be an important criterion when hiring new managers.[51] But managers have a responsibility to develop their listening skills and competencies. This section describes a more practical approach to developing and becoming a manager that listens.

Ask Clever Questions

We return here to the theme of questions since it is so important that it bears repeating. Poet Bob Hansson reflects on leadership and the importance of asking questions in the Swedish radio show *Seriously Talking*, 21 July 2018:

> It is said that yesterday's leaders were the best at answering, while the leaders of the future are the best at asking questions. And the number of questions a team asks each other is linked to the quality of their output. Questions allow people to be seen, and being seen makes people relax. And when we relax, our brains can function better.[52]

Given that talking is rewarded by organizations and their managers, it is a good idea to start listening by asking questions to coworkers and other important stakeholders. Asking questions is also a way for managers to help the organization reduce its risk-taking, as questions can reveal potential pitfalls and other risks.

Unfortunately, research shows that managers too rarely exploit the great potential of asking questions, thereby missing out on creating increased opportunities for learning, exchanging ideas, and improving relationships with coworkers.[53]

Skills in asking questions help to provide better support and *feedback* to coworkers. The answers to the questions increase the knowledge and understanding of coworkers' needs and how they experience their work. The knowledge can be used to develop strategies and activities that create the conditions for becoming a listening organization.

In principle, a manager should know something about each coworker's frame of reference—their background, the values that shaped them, etc. Indeed, many of us have at some point heard successful sports leaders tell us that one of the keys to the success of a team or an individual is that they know each athlete—they know their team.

At one point, one of us listened to a national alpine skiing coach who told us that he spends much time traveling to the families of national skiers, having coffee with their parents. The purpose is to investigate and try to understand everyone's frame of reference related to their background, conditions, and principles. A first thought is that this is impossible in an ordinary managerial job, and maybe it is. But our examples illustrate how important it is to get to know and listen to one's coworkers to create good conditions for reaching constructive solutions and development in organizations.

Give Feedback

Providing continuous feedback to coworkers is often highlighted in research as an activity and a tool to create happiness, well-being, increased trust, and opportunities for the personal development of coworkers.[54] The terms response and feedback are often synonymous and have several different definitions or interpretations. We have settled on the following definition used by Kentell and Wöhlecke-Haglund in their book *The Feedback (R)evolution*: "A description of what I perceive you to be doing and how what you are doing affects me".[55]

Feedback and listening are closely connected. Managers need to listen to provide feedback to coworkers. By listening and getting to know coworkers, a manager can become better at describing to other people how coworkers affect each other. This can make everyone work better together, enhancing the organization's success.

A Reflection from the Mission of Being a Manager

One of us, Anette, has years of experience being a manager. One of her insights is that most people have a huge desire to receive feedback and confirmation. Over the years, coworkers have pointed out that what they need more, above all, is positive affirmation. When we work as consultants and meet coworkers in organizations, we usually ask them if there is anyone in the room who feels as if they have received too much confirmation in their lives. Unsurprisingly, no one so far has received too much affirmation.

Buckingham and Goodall write in their article "The Feedback Fallacy" in the *Harvard Business Review* that it is important when giving feedback to first focus on what people do well and are good at. This is because our brains perceive negative criticism as a threat, which reduces brain activity and impairs learning ability. Therefore, focus on what works well in conversations with coworkers! In other words, avoid negative criticism, often called constructive criticism. This type of criticism rarely works constructively and as intended.[56]

Tom Peters, to whom we have referred earlier, says in his latest—and last—book that managers are generally bad at giving feedback. Peters points out:

In 9 out of 9.1 times, our ability to provide feedback is lousy.[57]

Peters's statement aligns with our understanding and experience too. Many managers know too little about their coworkers to provide relevant feedback. Encouraging and praising coworkers seems particularly difficult. This requires both humility and empathy, which increased listening makes possible. Managers are neither trained to listen nor trained to provide feedback. They are also likely to lack positive reinforcement from their managers, so the question is: Who should start?

Step Out of the Information Bubble!

Many managers enter little information bubbles and opinion corridors where they find people with similar opinions.[58] The entrapment in the information bubble results from overconfidence in oneself and one's information, combined with outdated ideas about leadership. In the bubble, warning signs are picked out, important facts are omitted, and the information one receives may have an overly optimistic bias. The bubble prevents a person from listening openly and constructively.[59] It acts as a shield that protects a person from essential but perhaps more negative and critical information, which one will need to grasp the complete picture of the organization's opportunities and obstacles.

One way to get out of one's information bubble is by creating an *ecosystem* for listening. Listening should be elevated as a higher-level activity to gain a holistic perspective.

By developing an ecosystem for listening, a person can get out of the information bubble. Following are some tips on how to do this:

- Be present and have an open dialogue with your coworkers. Meet with coworkers regularly, and follow your salespeople on sales trips while keeping it in mind to ask questions.
- Ask for reports on what your competitors are up to.
- Broaden the network you use to gather information.

- Ask your coworkers to assess your work continuously: What should I continue to do? What should I stop doing? What should I start doing or do a lot more of? The answers should be compiled and analyzed.
- Create structures and routines for listening so that everyone understands that you want to listen to them.
- Make space in your calendar to listen.
- Create the right conditions in your workspace for listening, for example, by furnishing it with two armchairs facing each other.

Beware of the Negative Impact of Power

Battlana and Casciaro argue in an article in the *Harvard Business Review* that it is time for managers to develop their humility and empathy since the sense of power tends to diminish the ability to do this.[60] They argue that the experience of having power, especially as a manager, makes one vulnerable to falling into two traps. One involves a sense of hubris, an exaggerated sense of self, or grandiosity. The second is self-centeredness, where power goes to the head of the manager. These two traps mean that the manager loses both himself or herself and others. By becoming aware of the downsides of power in leadership, ways can be found to counter both hubris and self-centeredness. Increased listening can be a way to develop both humility and empathy.

Humility is the antithesis of hubris and is a way to counteract it, while developing empathy can curb self-centeredness. To free yourself from hubris and self-centeredness, you must start by understanding your abilities, achievements, and limitations. Acting with humility means freeing yourself from negative pride and arrogance. You can develop your humility by starting to say "I don't know", asking more questions than giving answers, and creating structures or channels in your organization where you are given and allowed to listen to honest input from colleagues. Honest input comes from giving others space to speak and reducing your self-centeredness. You must also immerse yourself in your coworkers' work; listening is a good tool. Finally, you can try to find ways to reward humility in your organization.

Tom Peters's mantra over the years has been that the key to success is putting people first on the agenda, both as a manager and as an organization. In his latest book *Excellence Now*, Tom Peters highlights the link between success and humanism.[61] The book argues that humanistic leadership requires managers to listen to their coworkers and other stakeholders. An essential part of such leadership is precisely the ability to be humble and empathetic.

Developing empathy is one way to counteract self-centeredness. Oftentimes, a self-centered focus is an effect of managers feeling they have something to prove to themselves or others. This leads to all attention being focused on the self. However, empathy can be trained and developed by simply becoming a better listener.

I Think It Helps!

I, Anette, have had long managerial experience, but I read with some horror the results of experiments conducted in research to investigate how the sense of power affects behavior. This research shows that when the people participating in experiments are asked to think that they have power and are considered highly ranked in the organization, they tend to behave less politely, carefully, and attentively toward other people. They become more impolite, inattentive, and self-centered, and even a sense of hubris can arise.[62] I think, "Help—what have I demonstrated in my previous leadership roles?" Through introspection, I can probably think of a few instances where my self-centered focus has influenced social relationships negatively. I believe that I would have benefited from knowing more, there and then, about the impact that power has on my capacity for humility, empathy, and listening.

Summary: Become a Better-Listening Manager

- Let go of your ego and start taking an interest in your coworkers. Other people become more enjoyable when you get to know them deeper.
- Reduce the time you spend talking as well as focusing on yourself. Take a more subordinate role in conversations with coworkers and others.
- Listen fully and be present in the conversation.
- Keep track of your emotions while listening. Train your impulse control—do not interrupt before the coworker has finished speaking.
- Refrain from judging those you listen, and avoid being defensive.
- Practice waiting to provide your solutions to problems.
- Use the power of asking questions. Encourage coworkers to talk by asking open and probing questions.
- Dare to show yourself vulnerable and allow yourself to make mistakes.
- Work on your personal development.[63]

Chapter 6

Listening Coworkership

IN THE PREVIOUS chapter, we focused on managers and their responsibility for listening as part of organizational communication. Based on existing research, academic literature, education programs, and other organizational initiatives, one may think that it is primarily the responsibility of managers to ensure that communication and the working climate are of adequate standards. There seems to be an exaggerated belief in the importance of managers in the organization, at least in comparison to coworkers. However, since the beginning of the 21st century, there have been increasing talks about the importance and responsibilities of coworkers. Concepts such as *coworkership* are being introduced, and a new field of research and knowledge is emerging. The literature on coworkership clearly states that coworkers have a responsibility to simplify the work for managers and contribute to the development of the organization. Thus, supporting the manager in their work constitutes good coworkership.

Coworkers in a Post-Bureaucratic Organization

There is increasing evidence that a post-bureaucratic organization is replacing the traditional bureaucratic organization. This kind of organization is characterized by rules and a clear hierarchical structure in which one-way communication dominates and the focus is on transmission of information. That is, the information would be delivered by the immediate superior, which in turn received the information from his or her superior. The well-known sociologist Max Weber believed that bureaucracy, the structure and rules for governing an organization, was the best way to achieve efficiency because it made organizations predictable and orderly.[1] Most people are probably familiar with the downside of bureaucratic organizations. One of the main problems is that an overly bureaucratic organization is slow to change, often because coworkers are not mandated to act independently and must follow policies and specific rules. As a result, when a new situation arises, staff are not allowed to improvise and solve the problem.

DOI: 10.4324/9781003413486-6

In a post-bureaucratic organization, hierarchies are replaced by networks. This leads to a flatter structure and allows the organization to adapt more quickly to changes in the environment.[2] In turn, this requires that coworkers have the mandate to act on their own to resolve the unpredictable situations that arise.[3] A post-bureaucratic organization is therefore recognized by a decreased hierarchy as well as more outstanding teamwork, flexibility, coordination, and governance through dialogue, self-organized units, and decentralized decision-making.[4] Furthermore, to enable coworkers to become independent decision-makers requires shared power and distributed leadership.[5]

Distributed Leadership

Distributed leadership constitutes another way of examining how organizations can be managed and governed. As stated in previous chapters, in research and practice, leadership has been strongly linked to the manager as a person—one can even talk about manager-centrism. Research on leadership by Mats Alvesson and Martin Blom at Lund University, among others, shows that managers often have a false and inflated understanding of their importance for the organization's success.[6] One explanation for the discrepancy between managers' talk and practice is that they have a distorted view of the business, often overly optimistic, which can be explained by a low level of listening in the organization. Alvesson and Blom point out that there are other ways of managing organizations than the traditional view of the manager as the critical factor for the organization's success. Examples include leadership involving advice, support, coordination, encouragement, and feedback contributing to coworkers' productivity.

Another way to organize and lead for success is to include and understand coworkership. Leadership and empowerment can be viewed as two sides of the same coin, being closely related and interdependent. Velten, Tengblad, and Heggen argue that managers and coworkers have different roles and functions and that colleagues must understand and meet each other to succeed in this mission.[7] This means that coworkers must facilitate the manager to perform their tasks, just as managers need to facilitate coworkers and make them feel that their tasks are meaningful. English-speaking researchers use the terms "employee" or "follower" instead of "coworker".[8] While "employee" is a pretty neutral term, follower seems to reflect a notion of passive coworkers who follow strong managers and obey what the manager orders. In other words, follower as a concept assumes that managers are the ones who know best and the ones who tell the rest of the organization what to do. There is a clear power aspect here where followers give up their power to their manager.[9] Thus, when the term follower is used implicitly, there is little margin for listening. The focus is on the manager, who speaks by informing and giving instructions on how the work should be done.

Coworkership is based on the ideas of the Norwegian work-life researcher Einar Thorsrud, who believed that coworkers should have more freedom to influence their work situation and, at the same time, take responsibility for ensuring that the work is done effectively. Jan Carlzon, who advocated replacing the concept of a follower with that of a coworker, has played a significant role in this development, at least in Sweden. Carlzon pointed out early that the primary value creation occurs at the front line of operations where coworkers meet customers, e.g., when a passenger at Scandinavian Airlines meets a coworker.[10] Coworkership is a Nordic phenomenon based on more democratic and relationship-based leadership. It focuses on how we relate to our tasks, colleagues, and employers.[11] The concept emphasizes co-creation, i.e., coworkers actively lead the work.[12] So, instead of coworkers being seen as passive individuals who carry out the orders they are given, they are seen as independent, thinking, and wise individuals who can make good decisions.

Coworkership is ultimately about taking responsibility, which can be divided into three parts.[13] Firstly, responsibility is about doing what *is expected* of the professional role and job descriptions. Secondly, responsibility is about being *accountable* and acting professionally and ethically. This, in turn, requires that coworkers have the freedom to act. In a bureaucratic organization based on rules and guidelines, there is seldom room for coworkers to act independently. Thirdly, responsibility is about *taking the initiative and acting proactively*. In other words, coworkers reflect on what needs to be done and act on it, even if it is not expected of their job role. Finally, well-functioning coworkership requires that managers dare to relinquish duties and show that they trust coworkers' judgement as well as competence to solve problems independently.

Communicative Coworkership

Coworkership aims to involve coworkers and create more efficient and successful organizations. Once coworkership is established, there is a greater chance for coworkers to take responsibility and take the initiative. One area that is somewhat overlooked is the communicative duties of coworkers. In practice, much of an organization's strategic communication is carried out by coworkers internally and in their dealings with external parties such as customers, citizens, and users.

The concept of communicative coworkership was introduced to academia by Heide and Simonsson in 2011 in the article "Putting Co-workers in the Limelight".[14] The article points out that coworkers should be placed in the limelight, as they are crucial for the organization's success. However, coworkers are regularly taken for granted. It is too common that managers' believe that the organization's success is built on their strategic work. But in all the millions of micro-meetings, both internally and externally, coworkers manage to have macro-effects. For example, in the service encounter, a micro-meeting, the customers' experiences determine the level of service quality, as well as their trust in the organization.

The purpose of communicative coworkership is to offer a different understanding of coworkers than that of passive recipients of management and immediate supervisors of communication. The organization's strategies and brand are realized in the encounter between coworkers and customers, and relationships and reputations are built.[15] Coworkers also have an essential role in detecting signals of negative changes at an early stage inside or outside the organization.[16] Such information is precious for decision-makers who can, at best, act to reduce the impact of a crisis or even keep one from occurring. Although communicative coworkership is a competitive advantage, it has received far too little attention.[17]

Internal trust is crucial for coworkers to be willing to be ambassadors for the organization. Internal trust is built mainly by management and their immediate supervisor listening to coworkers. Even everyday conversations within the organization reinforce organizational identity. Nonetheless, managers withhold information or act unfairly.[18]

Communicative coworkership entails expecting coworkers to actively contribute to sharing knowledge with colleagues, including those in other departments. They should also contribute to a climate of open communication by not criticizing or punishing others who have different views and improve and develop external trust by treating customers well.[19]

It is possible to identify different communication roles that coworkers may have. In the report "Communicative Coworkership", Andersson, Heide, and Simonsson suggest three roles, as it is easier to distinguish between a limited number of roles.[20] Coworkers should take responsibility to:

- Contribute to a shared understanding and meaning
- Contribute to an open communication climate and the development of the business
- Contribute to reinforcing the trust and reputation of the organization

The researchers have deliberately chosen to use the word "contribute" to emphasize that the responsibilities are a joint process involving managers and coworkers. Leadership research also increasingly emphasizes that leadership is not linked to one person alone, i.e., the manager, but that it is a collective process.[21]

Listening constitutes an essential element of the three roles. To create shared understanding and meaning, coworkers must listen to each other, managers, and customers. Some shared understanding emerges only after listening and talking to different people.

An open communication climate is characterized by listening, and when people are willing and actively start listening to each other, trust is built. With increased trust, the open communication climate improves; everyone in an organization is responsible for creating and maintaining this.[22] However, it should be stressed that to take on the role of communicative coworkership, individuals need communication skills and mandates within certain limits to make independent decisions. It is also essential that reward systems are in place for those coworkers who take responsibility for a communicative coworkership.[23]

The Art of Distancing Oneself and Not Taking Responsibility

Hi! We remind you of your appointment on 14/10 at 09:45 AM, at the children's clinic. ONE close relative may accompany you, but no siblings. You cannot reply to this text message.

This was stated in a text message to Mats from a university hospital. An invitation had been sent out earlier, and the text message arrived a day before the visit. However, the text message did not contain enough information about the location and clinic. Once at the reception of the children's hospital, Mats pointed out to the receptionist that the text message lacked information about where the doctor's appointment would occur. The receptionist replied: "We are not in charge of the message service". Mats responded: "But don't you work here and have responsibility for passing on the feedback of patients?" The receptionist replied: "Well, actually— many persons have pointed out the same thing". Here is a clear example of when coworkers do not take a collaborative approach to listening and genuinely acknowledging customers. In this case, Mats' trust in the organization was not reinforced.

The Role of Coworkers as Listeners

In dealing with those that the organization serves, such as customers, patients, clients, or citizens, there are great opportunities for coworkers to fulfill several different roles or functions, especially in terms of communication. The skills and expertise of coworkers are significant organizational intellectual capital. In our experience, organizations do not sufficiently ensure that they have broad access to this capital.[24] In all organizations and mainly in customer-oriented organizations, the role of coworkers is often to listen to their managers, colleagues, partners, and customers. This means that coworkers have access to a significant source of information—information that is both important and interesting for the organization.

By listening and asking questions of the organization's coworkers, one gains access to their important knowledge. At the same time, coworkers feel validated, increasing their sense of purpose and motivation to continue listening to customers and colleagues. Intellectual capital must also be integrated and institutionalized in the organization's systems, routines, policies, and innovation work for it to be instructive and beneficial to the organization.

Coworkers as Communicators and Ambassadors

Many organizations have recognized the critical role of communicative cowork- ership, even those who are not full-time communicators. Communication research is also starting to take an interest in this, not least in the role of cowork- ers as brand ambassadors.[25] Research shows that when the general perception among managers is that coworkers must be fully controlled in what and how they communicate, coworkers are likely to act as a brand saboteur. Thus, creating an open, supportive, and inclusive communication climate is crucial.

The coworkers are also important points of interaction, as they meet the customers every day. Anna Tufvesson writes in her book *Active Coworkership* that as a coworker, one carries the organization's brand into every customer encounter and is paid to promote that brand.[26] Of course, a coworker must be given the conditions to do this. For coworkers to have the opportunity to create a positive experience, the individual coworker needs to have the will (understand why something is important), knowledge and time (how to do something and what to do), and mandate.[27] As mentioned earlier, coworkers' attitude and listening skills are linked to their willingness. If there is a lack of will, it may be because the organization's support systems are not working, and it is up to the customer-facing coworker to compensate for these deficiencies.[28]

Many organizations invest significant resources in gathering customer perceptions and opinions to understand their needs, wants, and service experiences better. Unfortunately, these resources are all too often wasted, usually because they ask the wrong questions, or ask questions but do not listen to their answers, or even worse, listen to the answers but do not act on what they hear.[29] Usually, the questions are phrased in a way that means the answers are useless in adding value to either the customer or the organization. More challenging questions need to be asked (for examples of such questions see Chapter 7).[30]

How to Listen to Criticism

One of the most challenging things to do as a coworker is to handle criticism from customers, users, citizens, or other organizational stakeholders. People in general find it difficult to take criticism because we perceive it as a threat to us as individuals. When we feel threatened, we unconsciously defend ourselves— "You made a mistake using the product". Or we blame others—"You should have told us about the problem earlier; now we cannot help you anymore". These are entirely natural human processes that occur automatically when we get a sense of being threatened. To avoid attacking or fleeing when a customer criticizes, we must first become aware of this reaction. We need to reflect on our behavior and talk to managers and colleagues about what happens with us when customers criticize us and how we can act in the future to avoid these negative feelings.

At the same time, we know that customers are very impressed when coworkers manage to handle and accept the criticism they receive. Customers who feel they are listened to and are respected gain increased trust in the organization. Gaining a high level of trust in the business is crucial for all organizations. It is also essential to understand that many hidden and valuable gems may appear in the criticism that is made. Criticism should be seen as an essential resource for changes and development in an organization. In a listening organization, it is well understood that taking criticism seriously is central to be a successful organization. At best, the organization can learn something new from the critique and adjust and adapt to improve service quality.

In the book *Ta skit! Och gör det till guld* (*Eng.* Take Shit! And Make into Gold), Annika R. Malmberg provides several practical pieces of advice for how organizations and coworkers can better develop how they handle complaints and criticism from customers.[31] Malmberg gives the following advice on how coworkers can positively handle negative comments:

The Art of Handling Criticism

- Show that you are listening and that you are genuinely interested.
- Show that you want to understand the scope of the problem—say—*I understand that you are annoyed.*
- Deliver a polite apology—as in—I am sorry that you feel this way.
- Fix the problem immediately or explain when it can be solved.
- Offer some coverage such as financial compensation, flower voucher, or cinema ticket.
- Thank the customer for providing the organization with valuable information that will be used to improve the business and the products or services.
- Provide feedback later, informing the customer that the procedures have changed and ensuring that the problem will not be repeated.[32]

This advice is like those that can be given for more excellent listening. It is about being sincere in your interest in listening, making time for it, and giving feedback. As mentioned earlier, a primary explanation for why coworkers do not feel seen and heard in organizations is that they do not receive feedback from their immediate manager—and the same is true for customers. If coworkers and customers are to continue to trust in and have a good relationship with the organization, they need to receive feedback.

Summary

- Empower coworkers to act and take responsibility for independently solving tasks and problems that arise.
- Coworkership entails that coworkers are seen as active, independent, thinking, and wise people who can make good decisions.
- Communicative coworkership means that coworkers have an important communicative duty where all micro-meetings internally and externally have macro-effects, such as increased trust for the organization.

- Coworkers have at least three different communication roles: a) contributing to a common understanding and meaning; b) contributing to an open communication climate; and c) developing the business and contributing to strengthening the organization's trust and reputation.
- Coworkers who meet customers need to develop their skills in handling criticism.

Chapter 7

How to Become a Strategic Listening Organization

IN PREVIOUS CHAPTERS of the book, we have shown that listening generally needs to be improved in organizations. Managers, coworkers, and organizational culture are some of the aspects highlighted as crucial for developing strategic listening. In this chapter, we take a holistic approach to organizing and structuring activities to create the right organizational conditions for strategic listening. First we start with a discussion of the problem of hoarding information with no intention to use it for organizational improvement and then continue with a presentation of a framework that can be used as a starting point for developing strategic listening.

Stop Information Hoarding!

Managers oftentimes state that they listen and that their organization is a listening organization.[1] On the other hand, listening is frequently mistaken as monitoring when organizations seek to obtain information on the perceptions and preferences of customers and coworkers[2] wherein the aim is to retrieve feedback from customers, coworkers, and other stakeholders in various ways through customer surveys, coworker surveys, and other forms of environmental monitoring. The common problem is that the information collected is rarely used to develop operations, new products, or services. Instead, the information gathered forms *information graveyards* where new information is continuously added. As described in previous chapters, the imperative problem is that management and managers are not *genuinely interested in* listening or making sweeping changes based on the collected information. Research also shows that organizations that actively conduct environmental monitoring spend most of their time gathering information and too little time analyzing it and using the information to improve, for example, service quality.[3] If this form of listening is to become something other than a pseudo-act, a genuine interest in other ways of understanding reality is required, as well as a willingness to change one's position.

Strategic listening is not about accumulating information. Neither is it about gaining the evidence to develop better arguments to persuade customers and

DOI: 10.4324/9781003413486-7

coworkers successfully. The goal of strategic listening, as we see it, is to listen to improve the organization, create dialogue, and develop mutually beneficial relationships internally and externally. To become a strategic listening organization, listening must be conducted *consciously, reflectively, targeted, and systematized.* This requires the involvement of all parts of the organization. As we pointed out earlier in this book, there must be a genuine interest in learning from the information that listening provides.

According to previous research, relatively little attention has been paid to what should be prioritized in organizations to achieve better and more systematized listening. Listening is still viewed as a *soft skill* and is often related to a person's personality. These so-called *soft skills* are commonly not particularly valued in organizations.[4] This may seem odd since research shows that soft skills such as listening, social competence, and empathy are some of the most valuable as well as necessary competencies for the success of today's organizations. Furthermore, it is often assumed that women have more outstanding capabilities in terms of soft skills than men. According to Barker and Watson, who wrote the book *Listen Up!*, men and women have different listening styles.[5] Men are considered more often than women to be action-oriented listeners, looking for information that can be useful to take action. Women tend to be more people-oriented in listening, looking for emotional messages and undertones in their communication. As a result, women are generally more interested in how messages are presented rather than the information being discussed. From this, it can be concluded that women generally seem to have more soft skills than men. However, it should be stressed that it is difficult to find research confirming that women listen differently from men and that the phenomenon can quickly become stereotypical. It is also important to point out that any differences between men's and women's listening should not be considered a matter of biological sex, but of the social norms of what is considered male and female behavior in a specific culture.[6]

A Framework to Become a Strategic Listening Organization

Our point of departure in this book is that an organization that seeks to improve strategic listening needs an overarching goal, such as becoming a customer-focused *organization*, meaning that all activities carried out in the organization should be prioritized from a customer point of view and this requires a customer-focused *management philosophy.*[7] We propose that a perspective of service logic should mark the management philosophy, a customer-focused perspective, which is particularly well suited to taking a holistic approach to strategic listening. As part of developing strategic listening in the organization, we have developed a framework (see Figure 7.1) to visualize some of the areas in an organization that are central to developing strategic listening.

The basis of the framework is service logic (see more later). The framework includes six areas of the organization that need to be prioritized to develop strategic listening. The different areas in the framework have no hierarchical order, and there are links between the different areas, as they are related and

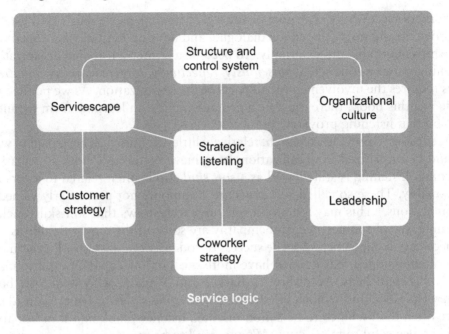

Figure 7.1 The framework of strategic listening.

interdependent. The framework is, of course, a simplification of reality. However, understanding and managing a complex reality can still be helpful.

Following, we review the basics of service logic and discuss how this logic can develop strategic listening. We briefly discuss the organizational areas covered in this book, such as leadership, human resource management, and culture. Service logic as such and the areas financial management, servicescapes, and customer strategies will be discussed in greater detail.

Management Philosophy: Service Logic

Strategic listening requires an explicit and sustained management philosophy. The term strategic as used in this book implies that this is an issue for the management level, which is usually responsible for developing the organization's strategies. Reviewing previous strategic or organizational listening research, it is not particularly extensive. On the other hand, much research has been conducted on interpersonal listening and, for example, the importance of listening to politicians, municipalities, and democracy. However, the research on listening only constitutes a tiny fraction compared to existing research on communication through speaking. So far, we have only found two books on listening within an organizational context. One is written by Laurie Lewis, and the other is by Jim Macnamara.[8] These books focus on *what* organizations should do and *how* they should do it to ensure strategic listening. Lewis and Macnamara point to the importance of developing a culture and structure and policies or procedures for listening—an aspect of organizational listening that we also think is very important. But in this book, we argue that there is a need for an even broader and more holistic organizational perspective compared to previous research.

We therefore advocate a management philosophy based on service logic. This logic will create good conditions for strategic listening. Service logic is a customer–focused management philosophy. In Figure 7.1, we show that service logic forms the base for the management of areas such as leadership, organizational culture, coworker strategies, customer strategies, etc., and the servicescape. We advocate that service logic as a management philosophy focusing on customer experiences and value creation is precisely what makes it such a good match for strategic listening—*a match made in heaven.*

Value creation and service theories have developed since the 1970s as a counterforce to the dominant perspective of goods logic.[9] Goods logic was developed within marketing during industrialization when organizations focused principally on the mass production of goods at low cost. Both goods logic and service logic have value and value creation as their key concepts but from two completely different points of departure.[10] Service logic presumes that the customer is the value creator and that value is created when a service is used. Thus, knowing your customer and their value-creating processes becomes central for management. Putting the customer experience at the forefront of the management philosophy as the starting point means working with an *outside-in perspective.* The organization needs to know its customers and understand how they create value.

The goods logic takes an opposed view of value creation, assuming that the value is created internally, meaning that the value is embedded in the good or service. Here, the customer's experience of using the product or service is not as necessary, as it is assumed that the value is already there. One could almost say that once the good is purchased, it can be equated with value destruction. Accordingly, the perspective of goods logic has an *inside-out approach*—put in simplistic terms. The perception is that "the organization knows best what the customer wants". Therefore, there is a lesser need to understand customers and their value-creating processes and no greater need to learn from and listen to customers' stories of their experiences.

Examples Goods Logic and Service Logic

A clear example of understanding the two perspectives of value creation is in the case of mobile phones, which can be understood as a product and a service. Initially, mobile phone manufacturers such as BlackBerry, Nokia, Motorola, and Ericsson emanated from the logic of the good. The focus was primarily on producing the most technologically advanced products on the market, and the products offered were presupposed by the possibilities offered by technology. On 9 January 2007, a paradigm shift occurred among mobile phone manufacturers when Apple launched its first iPhone.

The development of the iPhone, beginning in 2004, focused on users and their needs and experiences. This differed from the other manufacturers, who took an inside-out perspective, with the technologists and developers at the center. When the first iPhone was launched, it was not initially perceived as a threat to the market. The iPhone was more or less viewed as a toy that was no match for its competitors' technologically more potent products. But Apple had looked at various ways to make iPhone more user-friendly and had developed the phone from a user's perspective by listening to its users' needs.

It is important to remember that the perspective of goods logic, as a management philosophy, is by no means outdated. Even though we are a service society or a service economy, the perspective of goods logic is still pertinent in many organizations. In reality, many of these organizations are service firms, although they still understand value creation as an essentially internal matter.

From the service logic perspective, it becomes clear that customers need to be included in the service process, as customers influence their quality experience. In the end, it is the customers who determine whether the quality of a product or service is good. Organizations that are well acquainted with their customers and understand how they create value will be the winners.[11] By listening more to customers, organizations gain more knowledge and create opportunities to develop and maintain good customer relationships.

Thus, what advantages can the perspective of service logic offer in terms of opportunities to become a strategic listening organization? We argue that the customer orientation that characterizes the perspective of service logic requires the organization to listen to customers, coworkers, and other stakeholders. Service logic requires that listening should form the guiding principles in the organization. To become a successful customer-oriented organization, listening must increase internally and externally.

Next, we discuss each theoretical model's organizational areas to show how they can facilitate the ability to become a strategic listening organization.

Structure and Control Systems

Research on service logic emphasizes the importance of organizational structure and governance systems in achieving increased value creation. In contemporary research on organizational listening, the importance of a structured approach to listening is highlighted. However, there is little discussion of the importance of organizational structure or governance systems.[12] It is a shame since both are crucial in creating the right conditions for strategic organizational listening.

Organizational Structure

Christian Grönroos one of the world's most cited service management research-ers stresses the importance of well-thought-out organizational structures and governance systems. These must be designed to facilitate value creation both internally and externally.[13] Unfortunately, we often see that structures and gov-ernance systems hinder value creation and listening rather than support it. For example, overly hierarchical organizational structures or silo structures hinder listening, as they are designed to disseminate information from management to coworkers in the organization. The same is true of reward systems that focus on measuring and rewarding what managers and coworkers produce or perform rather than finding ways to reward listening.

Can an organizational structure be designed to foster listening and enhance value creation? The answer to this question is yes! The service logic points to the need to flatten organizations so that there are fewer levels of management and more responsibilities delegated to coworkers to ensure good value creation.[14] By delegating responsibility, coworkers can make decisions closer to the cus-tomer, wherever they are in the organization's structure. We must not forget that coworkers with customer contacts contribute significantly to value creation with customers. In many cases, this is crucial for the organization to ensure quality. In addition, it means that the rest of the organization should primarily support these coworkers.

The service logic assumes that the coworkers are empowered (see Chapter 6 on coworker leadership) to make decisions as close to the customer as possible, preferably directly when they interact with the customer. This enables them to act on what customers say in the interaction. This motivates coworkers to listen, as they know they have the *freedom of action* and *opportunities to act*. In addi-tion, a decentralized organization can allow for more cross-border collaboration to solve customers' problems, for example, if a coworker hears something from a customer that concerns another department in the organization.

A further important factor in achieving strategic listening is assigning greater responsibility for listening to specific functions. Many departments within an organization could be responsible for leading, supporting, and training in orga-nizational listening. However, we advocate that the communications department be given this responsibility. Communicators are the organization's communica-tion experts who not only produce content and messages and publish information themselves but also take responsibility for the organization's listening.[15] As we highlighted in the introduction, communication is about speaking (and inform-ing) and listening. In our experience, too many organizations lack a strategic, holistic approach to organizational listening. Much listening is going on, but a more systematic approach is often missing. Once communicators take responsi-bility for encouraging and creating routines and processes for strategic listening, they can face some challenges. Research conducted in the United States shows that communicators are well aware of the importance of listening but too rarely make listening a priority.[16] Reasons given for not prioritizing listening include that management does not value or want more listening, time constraints, and low coworker trust in management.

Control System

Economic governance systems also need to be adapted to support and promote listening. These may include governance systems relating to principles of resource allocation, productivity, measurement, and reward. Many organizations have an overly traditional and instrumental view of financial management systems. One challenge is that many financial management systems were initially developed for the manufacturing industry. However, they are also used in service organizations. This is problematic since the management systems were initially designed to control, monitor, and measure the production of goods. Consequently, traditional management systems focus on quantitative rather than qualitative measures, such as how many services have been performed or how many customers have been contacted throughout the week. In contrast, traditional management systems are less likely to examine how service users—customers—perceive the value or quality of the service.

Traditional governance systems therefore need to be reviewed, evaluated, and developed, as they often focus on the wrong things. In addition, financial management systems are critical because they shape and guide the organization's work in many respects. In the box that follows, we provide examples of questions that can be used to start the developmental work of control systems.

Questions to Start to Develop the Work of Control Systems

- Do we provide resources for activities that enhance the quality experience where listening is critical?
- Do we measure the quality of experiences for our customers?
- Do we know why customers are satisfied or dissatisfied with quality?
- Do we know which activities or behaviors create value for customers?
- Do we reward behaviors that increase the value creation for our customers?

These questions are not as easy to answer and measure compared to how easy it is to count, for example, the number of calls a customer service agent handles daily. This is undoubtedly a significant reason why traditional measuring methods are still utilized. But who said that development should be a piece of cake? Next we look at how you can work with resource allocation, productivity, measurement, and rewards to support strategic listening.

The issue of *resource allocation*, which takes place in the budget process, is a central control tool that governs what is fulfilled in organizations and is designed to critically review and evaluate whether the organization allocates resources in a way that creates value creation and listening conditions. To create the conditions for strategic listening, organizations must invest resources in all the organizational areas shown in the model earlier (see Figure 7.1).

Once the decision to become a strategic listening organization has been made, we suggest an initial focus on increasing the listening skills of staff. This can be done by training and recruiting personnel with the desired skills. It is also essential to invest resources in developing the technical support systems so that the organization can communicate with customers, for example, via social media, and to use technologies such as artificial intelligence (AI)–based text analysis of customer feedback.

How the organization views and understands *productivity* is essential to financial management systems. Often, productivity is viewed, more or less, to be the same as cost-effectiveness and therefore becomes an internal issue.[17] However, a perspective based in service logic, productivity is essentially an external issue, as customers influence productivity. The customers' perception of quality and value creation determines the organization's productivity. If customers perceive the organization's services as low or poor quality, productivity will decline. It is therefore a good idea to *listen to how customers* perceive the quality of the services. If an organization wants to maintain high productivity, it must listen to its customers.

The following control system to examine is the *reward system*. This system must be designed to promote value creation and increase customers' quality experience. Coworkers must be rewarded for behaviors, attitudes, and activities that enhance the customers' feeling of being listened to. The organization should reward coworkers who demonstrate listening skills internally and externally in various ways to promote value creation.

The same principles mentioned earlier must apply to measuring performance, i.e., to examine and measure customers' experiences of value creation and the internal processes and activities that lead to their experiences. The metrics that many organizations work with result from the design of control systems and can occasionally be viewed as close to customer-hostile. An example of this will be if customer service staff are evaluated based on the number of calls they answer in a working day rather than the quality of the calls. In other words, they do not measure the customer's quality experience, for example, whether the customer gets an answer to their question or how quickly the problem could be solved. Measuring performance in quantitative terms (i.e., how many or how much) encourages behaviors that make coworkers want to keep calls short so that they can answer as many calls as possible in a day. Many of us have probably experienced being mixed up within the organization or receiving the wrong help and therefore needed to call numerous times to solve our problem. While the calls are many and short, just as the organizations aim for, our experience of the quality of the conversations is anything but positive.

The experience of value creation by customers is referred to as *external efficiency*. A perspective based in service logic claims that the customer experience of value creation must be at the center of the measurement. However, this does not mean that measuring internal efficiency, usually cost-effectiveness, should not be done. Measuring external effectiveness must always come first, which is unfortunately not the case in many organizations. In summary, more qualitative methods are needed, and the reliance on quantitative measurements must be reduced.

Customer Strategies

We refer to all strategies and actions aimed at supporting and empowering customers to make their voices heard as customer strategies. This also includes the organization's interest in and commitment to engaging and listening to customers. Following we address three areas that are important to focus on in the customer strategy to become a strategic listening organization:

1. Customer dialogue
2. Customer surveys
3. Critical comments

Customer Dialogue

For organizations that want to develop their listening functions, customer dialogue is one of the most critical areas to develop. Organizations should start by actively inviting customers to communicate through various communication channels. It is then essential that the organization is simultaneously prepared to receive and respond to what customers say through these different communication channels.

Unfortunately, research shows that the listening generally taking place in organizations' communication channels, such as face-to-face service encounters, on social media, in citizens' councils, and in other dialogue forums, is too instrumental.[18] Many times, this type of listening is done solely to serve the purpose and goals of the organization. In other words, the organization has an inside-out perspective. There is then only one winner, and the opportunity for communication based on a *win-win* perspective is at risk. Strengthening customer dialogue requires designing processes and systems that enable customers to have their say while ensuring the organization has the resources and skills to respond to and address what is being communicated in the different channels. Unfortunately, too many of us have experienced that we, as customers, communicated our issues and views to organizations without any reaction or response. This gives us the feeling that no one seems interested in what we have to say, as we rarely get feedback on what we have asked or comments provided.

Customer Surveys

Another area where organizations need to improve is *customer research*. There is no shortage of customer surveys, but rather an increase in them. In general, organizations spend too much time and resources on customer surveys of various kinds, which, unfortunately, often need to be improved. This waste of time and money is usually because the wrong questions are being asked, and the answers do not reveal what is problematic in the relationship between the organization and customers. Or many relevant questions are asked, but no one listens to the answers. In the worst case, someone listens to the answers but does not make changes based on what is communicated, even when it is warranted. Many organizations also need to be able to communicate to their customers what they have developed and improved through the feedback they received from them.[19]

For example, we only are able to leave the health center after we receive an email with questions about how our visit was experienced, or we are expected to press a button with a happy or sad face as we pass through security at the airport. Nowadays, at least, we have stopped filling in these surveys and do not press any buttons with happy or sad faces either. We, and many people with us, only participate in some of these surveys because there are too many of them, and we hardly ever get any feedback. Many customer investigations are survey-based or entirely mechanical, like when an AI robot calls back after a completed call with customer service. Instead, organizations should invest more resources in qualitative research, such as individual customer interviews, focus groups, and observations. At the same time, all coworkers must be educated and trained to constantly examine how customers experience the organization's services and value creation.

Organizations also need to get better at asking *sharp questions*. Customer responses often need to provide more information for managers in organizations to see problems, and then the questioning does not lead to potential development either. Questions are too often too instrumental, a little too "nice", and phrased in a way that challenges neither the customer nor the organization. More incisive questions need to be formulated to identify areas for development. These should be questions that allow customers to have their say on what is working but give their views on what they feel *is not* working in the organization's services and offerings. The box that follows contains suggestions for more incisive questions.

Sharp Questions for Customers

- Are you satisfied with your experience with us? Why or why not?
- What do we do or not do that causes frustration?
- If you could make a wish, what is the one thing we absolutely must not stop doing?
- Name ONE thing we can do better!
- Is there anyone among us who has impressed you?
- Why did you become a customer of our organization in the first place?
- Why do you choose to be our customer?
- Is there anyone inside or outside our industry that you believe we can learn from?
- What would you say if someone asked you about us?

Many other questions can be used to determine what the organization is good at and could be better at. The important thing is that organizations seek answers to the question WHY something works or does not work. Obviously, the questions need to be adapted to the context in which the organization finds itself, or they need to be omitted because they are irrelevant or incorrectly asked. For public organizations, questions based on a traditional customer relationship are inappropriate and need adjustment.

Critical Comments and Complaints

Another area that needs special attention for an organization to become a strategic listening organization is the ability to deal with *critical customer feedback*. To be curious, listening to and addressing critical feedback is extremely important and influential in enhancing value creation. Moreover, criticism is an excellent source of innovation and development. Criticism does not, of course, only come from customer surveys. They appear everywhere, both internally and externally. In addition, a listening organization should work progressively to stimulate criticism. This is because research shows that, regardless of the sector, 95 percent of those dissatisfied with an organization choose not to voice their opinions.[20] In light of this, internal processes, systems, and procedures are needed to stimulate critical feedback and staff with listening skills. In addition, an organization that is interested and willing to take on what is voiced is needed to develop its activities.

Becoming good at stimulating critical feedback and dealing with it is a relatively simple way to be perceived as a listening organization by coworkers, customers, and other stakeholders. However, we may have to admit that listening to criticism is challenging. Our defense mechanism often kicks in with full force when we encounter someone who wants to complain about something, and listening can become entirely unattainable. Knowing this, organizations first need to educate and train their coworkers to listen to criticism and show that they are happy for customers to give them their more critical views. On this note, the book *The Complaint Is a Gift* shows how complaints and criticism benefit the organization's value creation and innovation.[21]

It is also important to emphasize that in some situations, one has to stop listening. This is particularly true with complaints. There are times when customers persist in their criticisms to have their problems solved. At such times, there is an expectation that if the organization listens to them, they will get what they want. Such an expectation of listening generally cannot and should only sometimes be met by the organization. In other words, there are instances when we *cannot* and *should not* go the customer's way. One example is organizations making government decisions that are only sometimes positive for those who receive them. Of course, we can listen to customers' objections and comments on the regulatory decision and then try to explain why it turned out the way it did. But that is where it stops. We cannot listen indefinitely because the decision will not change no matter how much we listen. During these circumstances, it is better to be very clear in your communication and, if possible, find ways to respectfully explain why the decision is the way it is and why it stands. In other words, finding customer-empathetic ways to say no is essential.

Customers Know Best (Usually)

Customers are often better at developing the organization than the organization itself.[22] There are several reasons for this, such as the fact that customers are more creative because they live close to their context and know what creates value for them. They therefore see problems much earlier than managers in organizations. In addition, many decision-makers and organizations often become "insular", i.e., they start from an inside-out perspective, limiting their ability to innovate. There is thus a strong case for listening to customers to achieve more incredible innovation and development. The challenge is that managers in organizations seem to wait for the complaints to come. Unfortunately, this is a fallacy—even minor criticisms that pop up here and there among various coworkers can be early warning signals of an impending challenge or crisis. These weak signals at a micro level can impact a macro level, i.e., if the minor complaints are not dealt with, the result can be a gradual loss of trust in the organization.

Leadership

A crucial prerequisite for achieving strategic listening in an organization is that management decides on a strategy where listening is explicit and considered necessary for the organization. Number one is to decide within the organization that listening is essential and should be used more strategically. The strategy should state that the listening organization is a guiding idea for all coworkers while also describing strategic listening and its objective. Once such a decision has been taken, management must demonstrate that it is interested in and values listening to coworkers, customers, and other stakeholders. Coworkers need to feel and experience that they are being genuinely listened to by management and receive feedback on the fact that what is being voiced is considered. This *does not* mean that everyone always gets what they want, but coworkers and customers should *feel they are being listened to* and receive some response to what is being voiced. This is why it is so important that the feedback of listening takes place, as well as that information and views of coworkers are considered.

The previous research we reviewed for writing this book suggests that managers spend far too little time listening.[23] Talking is utterly dominant in managers' communication, a relationship we believe needs to change. Furthermore, in the previous chapter on leadership, we pointed to several things that required improvement. In addition to what we said in the previous chapter, we would like to emphasize some factors that may be the most important.

Exercising Communicative Leadership

In recent years, the concept of *communicative leadership* has been highlighted, and many Swedish organizations have actively been working to develop the knowledge and skills of leaders in communication. The concept has existed in Nordic countries since the 1990s. It focuses on the need for dialogue and sensemaking between managers and coworkers to establish increased commitment and trust. In the thesis, *The Communication Challenge: A Study of Manager-Coworker Communication in a Modern Organization*, Charlotte Simonsson examines the increased demands for communication in organizations and the communication challenges managers face.[24] The thesis shows that communication is often seen and practiced as disseminating messages from a manager to coworkers rather than exercising communicative leadership. When the study managers were invited to dialogue, it was often done superficially, and the dialogue could have been more genuine.

Communicative leadership is a manager who "engages coworkers in dialogue, provides and seeks feedback, involves coworkers in decision-making, and is perceived as open and present".[25] It becomes clear that communicative leadership is the same as a listening manager. A manager who engages in dialogue, provides feedback, and involves coworkers in decision-making must also be a good listener. Only when leaders have begun to listen to coworkers and acknowledge them as necessary can sufficient trust be established for genuine dialogue.

Act as Role Models or "Walk the Walk"

It is described as a frequent problem in organizations that managers "talk the talk but do not walk the walk". In other words, managers are generally better at talking about what should be done but worse at acting on what they talk about. Therefore, managers need to start to listen and not just talk about how important it is for others in the organization to listen. Managers have an essential role in setting an example of a strategic focus on listening. However, not all managers seem to understand that they are viewed as role models by others. Perhaps more importantly, they do not always take responsibility for their actions as role models.

We will now show what we mean with an example. We have worked as consultants in various organizations with training courses on the theme "we will become more customer-oriented". Many times, unfortunately, managers have been too preoccupied with their phones or computers, occasionally, leaving the training room with an excuse such as that they need to "make important phone calls". But what could be more important than showing coworkers that training on becoming more customer-oriented is essential? By listening with interest to the person invited to hold a training session on the topic? It may seem like a small matter, but it is actually symbolic. Coworkers are curious about what is going on and the norms. They are constantly looking to their managers to ensure they understand what is essential in the organization and how to act on what appears necessary. This investment in training is completely wasted if the manager acts the way the example suggests. What the manager is saying with his or her actions is clear—customer orientation is not essential in our company. Seeing how managers do things and then mimicking their attitudes and behaviors becomes an *easy way to get it right*. That said, managers who take responsibility for acting in line with the management philosophy are needed.

Create Forums for Informal Contact between Management and Coworkers

Research suggests that visibility and communication between management and coworkers are crucial to establishing internal trust.[26] As early as 1938, Chester Barnard pointed out in his book *The Executive Functions* the importance of informal communication in an organization. To increase internal trust and listening, various forums should be provided where informal communication between management and coworkers can occur. For example, management team members should regularly be out in the field, informally talking to and listening to coworkers and customers. In the book *Hug Your Customers*, Jack Mitchell, who owns and operates several clothing stores in the United States, describes how the job descriptions for all managers include being out in the field continuously.[27] This is designed to get close to both the coworkers in the stores and customers to understand how to create value for them. Mitchell asks: How will a purchasing manager even understand what our customers want if they are away from interacting with them occasionally? A manager cannot simply get that knowledge by sitting at their desks. Manager visits also provide an opportunity to interview coworkers who meet the company's customers daily about their experiences of the market. This provides managers with up-to-date and vital information that can be taken to the management team meetings.

Moreover, when management genuinely listens, coworkers greatly appreciate it, reinforcing internal trust. Of course, it is also possible to build forums on internal social media as a channel where the management team is available to listen to thoughts, suggestions, and ideas and answer coworker questions.

Personal Development

Based on the work of Swiss psychologist and philosopher Jean Piaget, scientists long believed that human development was complete after adolescence. In contrast, psychology professor Robert Kegan has identified five stages of how humans develop throughout life:

1. *The impulsive stage:* Two to six years.
2. *The need-centered self:* Six years to late adolescence.
3. *The socialized self:* Late adolescence and beyond. In this stage of life, group identity and being part of a group are valued and essential. In the center is oneself, fitting in and performing to impress others.

4. *The self-authoring self*: This takes place for some people in their 40s, as many people go through some life crisis, for example, due to age or divorce. With these types of crises, the individual starts disengaging from the group and becomes more and more of an independent thinker who follows their internal compass but at the same time remains open to taking in others' perspectives.

5. *The integrated self*: This is a stage of life that some people reach in their 70s when they change in terms of depth and take responsibility for a more significant cause.

Some people remain in the third stage, and those with a strong focus on the self are likely to be poorer listeners than those who have entered the self-perceived self.

If managers are to become better listeners, they should be allowed to work on their personal development. It is probably not a bad idea to provide all managers with some form of coaching in their role, whatever their level—someone to listen to them as they suffer, just like other colleagues, from a lack of attention and affirmation. They feel alone in their role, sometimes even more than their colleagues. Ensuring coaching, which often means an opportunity for a personal development journey, creates better conditions for greater empathy and an increased ability to provide feedback to coworkers.

Creating a Structure for Listening in Meetings

It is crucial to create meeting structures that encourage better listening. Tourish and Robson emphasize that management teams and other leadership groups need to focus more on the upstream negative information, i.e., critical information or deviating from conventional wisdom.[28] Such information often contains essential aspects that should be considered in decision-making. Tourish and Robson suggest that management teams regularly ask themselves several questions (see the box that follows).

Sharp Questions for the Management Team

- What problems have come to our attention since the last time we met?
- How do you find the cooperation with me as a manager?
- What criticisms have been made of the decisions we have taken?
- What are coworkers and customers satisfied with at the moment?
- How is the amount of positive and negative criticism distributed in the feedback we have received over the past week?
- Is the criticism justified and, if so, entirely or partly?
- How should we act on the criticism that has come to our attention?

Organizational Culture

Strategic listening is based first and foremost on the organization's culture, constituting the most critical area of our model. An organization that decides to develop strategic listening must welcome and accept values and goals and an identity that accompanies authentic, ethical, and goal-driven listening.[29]

Laura Lewis argues that there are four basic assumptions that organizations should make to develop a strategic listening culture:

1. Listening is not a gift to those you listen to—it is a strategic task for those who listen.

2. Listening effectively, continuously, and strategically is a prerequisite for the organization's survival and the most critical ingredient for success.

3. Strategic listening requires that systems, processes, and structures are designed to gather data, information, and perspectives to build knowledge.

4. Strategic listening is best achieved by analyzing the organization's listening capacities and "blind spots"—areas not usually paid particular attention to. This is to strategically develop listening systems, structures, and processes that, in turn, contribute to a culture where listening is present throughout the entire organization.[30]

Developing an Open Culture

The organizations that can be described as communicative have in common that the culture is perceived as open and that coworkers do not feel anxious or afraid to express dissenting opinions or criticism. Therefore, for increased and strategic listening to be possible, the organizational culture must be open and supportive.[31]

Organizational culture comprises fundamental assumptions, dominant thoughts, ideas, values, and norms. These tell managers and coworkers what is expected of them and set the framework for how they interact. A premise of an open organizational culture is that top management believes that openness is essential and then demonstrates in various ways that they genuinely believe in openness. Again, as in parenting, leaders must set an example and seek coworkers' voices. An open organizational culture is impossible without trust between top management, managers, and coworkers. And the way to build trust is to be open with each other. When there are conditions for an open organizational culture, there are also conditions for coworkers to feel psychological safety. This safety prevails when coworkers can express themselves freely without fear of various forms of punishment. We mentioned in Chapter 3 on listening and culture that an open communication climate requires courageous leadership in which managers can show themselves as vulnerable and fallible. When managers dare to do so, trust within the organization increases. In other words, showing vulnerability is nothing for cowards—it takes a great deal of courage.

One way to open the organizational culture to listening is to introduce a routine of starting meetings by *checking in on* what everyone is working on, what feels good and fun, and what feels awkward. This is a great way for colleagues to open up and increase their understanding of each other.

Another way is to introduce *retrospective meetings*, where the aim is for all participants to stop and reflect on what they have been through. One of the purposes of this reflection is to allow coworkers to think about and talk about their experiences. Another aim is to use everyone's reflections to increase knowledge and understanding of the organization's opportunities and challenges to better work on the development of the organization.

Paying Attention to the Politics of Listening

Strategic listening has a political dimension that should be addressed. It is mainly about how organizations choose to listen to some people and not to others. The act of not listening becomes political, whether the organization intends it or not.[32] Furthermore, Macnamara argues that organizations should address internal political issues surrounding listening.[33] This includes examining whether there are any signs of selective listening, such as listening more to some and not to others, and why this is the case. In this way, an organization can become more open about the internal political game and take steps to balance listening to different groups, both internally and externally.

There is also another internal political dimension that should be considered to develop a listening culture. It is common for coworkers to choose not to bring bad news to their managers because, in their experience, managers react negatively to such information. Either the coworker who delivers the bad news suffers criticism through managers showing frustration or anger when listening to negative information or managers meet the information with total silence. The news is buried and never discussed again. Both of these ways lead to the development of a fear of passing on more damaging information to managers, thereby running the risk of closing rather than opening the culture of listening while a culture of silence develops (see Chapter 3).

Coworker Strategies

The service logic's clear customer orientation means that the employee perspective is central and must be ensured. Coworkers have the best knowledge of the market: how customers create value and how organizations can facilitate this. Knowledge is obtained since they devote their days to listening to customers. Paul Warner puts this very aptly: *if you want to hear the voice of the customer—listen to your people.*[34] Coworkers with a high level of customer contact can share their knowledge of the customer experience and their feedback with the organization.

Several years ago, one of us wrote an opinion piece entitled "Staff More Important Than Customers".[35] By that, we mean that organizations with high-value-creation targets must clean up their act. That is, if you want your coworkers to be responsive and listen to the needs and descriptions of customer experiences, your organization must start by listening to its coworkers.

Making Use of the Customer Knowledge of Coworkers

All coworkers possess a wealth of knowledge about the people they serve—internal and external customers—not least through listening to others.[36] The knowledge of customers and the market that coworkers with external customer contact have is particularly important to take care of to learn and develop the organization. However, research by Stephen Tax and Stephen Brown shows that many organizations do not possess effective ways of working or do not have systems to ensure that customer and market knowledge is captured.[37] The same research suggests that most customers do not feel satisfied with how coworkers deal with complaints, and their negative feelings are reinforced after contact with the organization. The dissatisfaction, in turn, leads to increased conflicts with customers, reducing trust in the organization. Tax and Brown emphasize that organizations need to put more resources into developing the abilities of coworkers to deal with complaints, including training them in the art of listening better.

With her previous work experience in management, Anette testifies that coworkers such as frontline staff are rarely (if ever) invited to management team meetings to share their knowledge of customers and the market that this group has. Some knowledge is very important when developing service proposition or when other service developments are to be discussed within management. Organizations need to find different forums for more people to share this knowledge. Internal focus groups, dialogue forums, and technical support systems can access and disseminate invaluable customer and market knowledge in the organization.

Against this background, we suggest: *Valuing the golden eggs* in your organization—the people who typically have a lower status but have contacts in the organization or have many meetings with customers or other stakeholders such as citizens or users—they can be the path to success!

Stimulate Listening

The organization needs to create activities that stimulate the behaviors of coworkers to increase interest in listening internally and externally. Motivation and commitment to listening can be created by working in different ways in the organization to provide feedback on an ongoing basis. People who are listened to and given feedback or coaching have an increased interest in learning and personal development.

Increased Support for Internal Communication

Continuously working on improving listening in organizations is an opportunity for internal communicators to make their functions meaningful. They can work to encourage dialogue and to make their voices heard, even if they want to voice criticism upward in the organization. Some suggested activities include organizing larger meetings internally to discuss different issues; organizing meetings between management and coworkers; holding interactive online sessions, listening lunches, and anonymous coworker surveys; and stimulating suggestions and ideas. Those responsible for developing and directing an organization's listening need to start to support and coach managers so that they become better at seeking coworkers' views and making sure they answer the questions that coworkers have.[38]

Train and Recruit for Listening

It is also a matter of training and recruiting staff who can develop and manage the systems for listening. In other words, it is about *listening*; monitoring; analyzing; and responding to comments, questions, complaints, and suggestions through the organization's communication channels.[39]

Furthermore, it is also necessary to ensure that the organization has the skills and technology to analyze text to see opportunities and changes in incoming emails, letters, complaints, and other social media forums. But it is also essential that there are staff resources to work on interviews, focus groups, conducting customer journeys, and analyzing what is happening on social media.

Servicescape: A Listening Landscape

All interactions in an organization, both internally between employees and externally between employees and customers, take place in a physically or digital location. This place is in service research called the *servicescape*. It includes a variety of resources—physical, social, and digital. The physical resources include the interior of the place: its design, technical tools, signage, light, sound, and smell, but also social resources, such as the people with whom coworkers and customers interact in the landscape. Today's digital servicescapes are mainly about digital resources such as websites, social media, and various technical systems. For example, the energy company EON has a system they call "Brand Inside" where the management can actively communicate with the staff at the customer center. This communication forms an essential basis for management decisions. Within EON there is a perception that the staff at the customer center provide quick insight into how customers perceive the organization. The customer center at EON thus has an explicit mandate to listen to customers.

Service research shows that a servicescape is a place of interaction and value creation that significantly impacts people's experiences.[40] It is therefore essential that the landscape be designed to support customers' value-creation processes. But it should be easy to create value in the locations where the organization meets its customers. We know that listening contributes to value creation by increasing trust and strengthening motivation, engagement, and the relationship between the organization and people. It is therefore interesting to ask whether organizations can design a servicescape in a way that creates the conditions for good listening. Of course, the answer is yes. The servicescapes can be designed in a way that considers opportunities for listening.

More needs to be found in existing research on servicescape and listening. However, in his book *Organizational Listening*, Macnamara points out that the organization needs technology of various kinds that supports listening in different ways, especially large-scale listening.[41] For example, there is a need for technical analysis tools that can be used to make sense of the information and data collected, as well as other technical support systems to follow the digital footsteps of customers. Websites, social media, and other analog and digital communication channels should be designed for listening by being open and interactive. If one is open to dialogue, there must be a recipient of what is said in these interactive channels.

However, many of us, unfortunately, have experience posting messages or questions on various social media or other communication channels to organizations without hearing a word from them. Therefore, we advise taking inventory of the various resources in the organization's servicescape to ensure that these are designed and crafted to support listening. Many of us desperately search various websites for such simple things as company contact details. Sometimes the thought crosses our minds that some companies avoid contact with their customers. They do not want to engage in dialogue and listen to them. Another problem is that organizations need to understand the value of designing their more physical customer environments in a way that encourages listening. Environmental issues, such as high noise levels, confined spaces, or large open areas, often make it difficult for coworkers to listen and for customers to have their say.

The Way Forward

We have reached the end of this book, and it is time to discuss a way forward. But what does the way forward look like? The main message of our book is that to become a strategic listening organization, management must start deciding to invest in developing the organization's strategic listening functions. Of course, if management is not interested in listening, one can still start improving the organization's strategic listening. Although we are fully aware of the complexities of developing an organization's strategic listening, it is essential to start with small steps forward in each strategic direction. South African Archbishop Desmond Tutu is reputed to have said: *there is only one way to eat an elephant—one bite at a time*. By this, he meant that when we face something that feels insurmountable or even impossible, we can still succeed by moving forward gradually. Furthermore, the American organizational psychologist Karl E. Weick wrote an article entitled "Small Wins" in 1984, in which he emphasized that the only way to deal with complex and significant challenges is to devise a *small-wins strategy*.[42] Such a strategy should consist of smaller sub-goals that, when achieved, demonstrate tangible progress for managers, coworkers, customers, and so on. Over time, these incremental successes will form a pattern of success that will make even more people want to follow suit and start investing in improving strategic listening. One can start small in a department, unit, or team. For example, start by introducing a check-in routine at meetings, where everyone is briefed on what to do and their challenges. This will give everyone a chance to speak, and the rest of the meeting will be used to pay attention to gaining a greater insight into each coworker's work situation. Other practices can also be put in place to promote listening in the organization, which is likely to have ripple effects on other parts of the organization. From there, the top manager will be calling to ask what is going on and be ready to jump on the listening bandwagon!

Endnotes

Preface

1 Stein (2017)
2 Carlzon and Dyberg (2021, p. 89)

Introduction

1 Daimler (2016, p. 5)
2 Sinek (2011)
3 Qin and Men (2022)
4 Langlinais et al. (2022)
5 Pery et al. (2020), Ruck (2021), Lewis (2019)
6 Zerfass and Sherzada (2015)
7 Lewis (1999)
8 Schwarz et al. (2021)
9 Zerfass et al. (2020)
10 Zerfass et al. (2021).
11 Carnegie (1936)
12 Lewis (2019)
13 Macnamara (2022)
14 Itani et al. (2019), Castleberry et al. (1999)
15 Jonsdottir and Fridriksdottir (2020)
16 Schramm (1948)
17 Schweidel and Moe (2014)
18 Macnamara (2016b)
19 Carlyle (1904)

Chapter 1

1 Nichols and Stevens (1957)
2 Carnegie (2017)
3 Carnegie (2017, p. xiv)
4 Burleson (2011)
5 Manusov (2020)
6 See for example Thorsell (2016)
7 Salisbury and Chen (2007)

8 Rönnberg (2015)
9 Hurley and Walczak (2020), Burleson (2011)
10 Carnegie (2017)
11 www.drive.se/kompetens/att-lyssna-en-underskattad-och-outnyttjad-resurs
12 Carey (2009)
13 Bavelas et al. (2000)
14 Yngve (1970)
15 Manusov et al. (2020)
16 Itzchakov et al. (2018)
17 Rogers and Farson (1957)
18 Rogers (1961)
19 Kriz et al. (2021)
20 Resnick (2019)
21 Lindeblad (2021)
22 Robson (2019)
23 Purdy (1991, p. 4)
24 Buber (1923/1994)
25 Gordon (2011)
26 Buber (1998)
27 Murphy (2021)
28 Patterson (2019)
29 Tufvesson (2017)
30 Ås (1990)
31 Boorstin (1963/1985)
32 Lewis (2019)
33 Alvesson (2022)
34 Sahay (2021)
35 Agarwal (2020)
36 Patterson (2019)
37 Covey (2022)
38 Renander (2010)
39 Psykologbyrån, podcast, September 2018.
40 Rosenberg (2015)
41 The *Love and Therapy* podcast with psychologist Daniella Gordon, 27 November 2021
42 Kåver and Nilsonne (2007)
43 Brown (2018)
44 Carlzon and Dyberg (2021)
45 Clarke and Eddy (2017)
46 Kahneman and Tversky (1979)
47 Alvesson and Spicer (2017)
48 Robson (2019)
49 Coleman (2022)

Chapter 2

1 Nichols and Stevens (1957)
2 Peters and Waterman (1982)
3 Peters and Waterman (1982, p. 196)
4 Macnamara (2016b)
5 Macnamara (2016b)
6 Macnamara and Gregory (2018)
7 Ruck et al. (2017), Ruck (2016)
8 Rashid (2021)

 9 Bornemark (2018)
10 Macnamara (2022)
11 Cole (2011)
12 Grant (2021)
13 Yip and Fisher (2022)
14 Yip and Fisher (2022)
15 Lewis (2019)
16 Macnamara (2016b)
17 Wadström et al. (2017)
18 See for example Clausewitz (1997)
19 Whittington (2001)
20 Pettigrew et al. (2006)
21 Mintzberg (1973)
22 Mintzberg et al. (1976)
23 Mintzberg et al. (1976), Weick (1995)
24 Rumelt (2022)
25 Weick (2020)
26 Smircich and Stubbart (1985, p. 734)
27 Weick (1995, 1998, 2002)
28 Johnson et al. (2003)
29 Jarzabkowski et al. (2021)
30 Jarzabkowski et al. (2007)
31 Beard and Bodie (2014)
32 Mower (2020)
33 Lipetz et al. (2018)
34 Rogers and Roethlisberger (1952)
35 Ramsey and Sohi (1997)
36 Lloyd et al. (2015)
37 Amin et al. (2011)
38 Schwartz (1998)
39 Macnamara (2016b)
40 Lewis (2019)
41 Lewis (2019, p. xvi)
42 Zuboff (2019)
43 Splitter et al. (2021), Whittington (2019), Whittington et al. (2020)
44 Pery et al. (2020)
45 Bergeron and Laroche (2009)
46 Levinson et al. (1997)
47 Kirtley Johnston and Reed (2017)
48 Pery et al. (2020)
49 Lipetz et al. (2018)
50 Chiang et al. (2020)
51 Norinder (2019)
52 See Brandebo (2021), Bringselius (2021)
53 Pery et al. (2020)
54 Castro et al. (2018)
55 Alvesson and Spicer (2017)
56 Ewerman (2015)
57 Browne and Nuttall (2013)
58 Canel et al. (2022)
59 Statskontoret (2015)
60 Kristensson et al. (2014)
61 Heide and Simonsson (2019)

Chapter 3

1 Carlzon (2001, in original 1985)
2 Grönroos (2015)
3 Alvesson and Sveningsson (2016)
4 Bang (1999)
5 Peters and Waterman (1982)
6 Deal and Kennedy (2020, in original 1982)
7 Smircich and Calás (1987)
8 Smircich (1983)
9 Smircich (1983), Alvesson and Sveningsson (2016), Alvesson (1995)
10 cf. Neill and Bowen (2021a, 2021b)
11 Cardon et al. (2019)
12 Cardon et al. (2019)
13 Morrison and Milliken (2000)
14 Morrison (2014)
15 Morrison and Milliken (2000)
16 Edmondson (2019)
17 Edmondson (2019)
18 Morrison and Milliken (2000)
19 cf. Tourish (2005), Tourish and Hargie (2004)
20 Glauser (1984)
21 Alvesson (2022)
22 Senge (1990)
23 Edmondson (2019)
24 Burrell and Morgan (1979)
25 Deetz (2000)
26 Christensen and Christensen (2022)
27 Kish-Gephart et al. (2009)
28 Helms and Haynes (1992)
29 Gans and Zhan (2022)
30 Bragg (2007)
31 Edmondson (2019)
32 Pery et al. (2020, p. 167)
33 Edmondson (1999, 2003a, 2003b, 2019)
34 Kahn (1990)
35 Potipiroon and Ford (2021)
36 Wendelheim and Rodell Lundgren (2021, p. 15)
37 Telléus (2020)
38 Wendelheim and Rodell Lundgren (2021, p. 15)
39 Wendelheim and Rodell Lundgren (2021, p. 22)
40 Brown (2015)
41 Wendelheim and Rodell Lundgren (2021)
42 Excerpt from interview with Lena Eriksson 2021–09–20 within the research project Communicative Public Organisations conducted by Mats Heide, Charlotte Simonsson and Rickard Andersson during the period 2020–2022 at Lund University.

Chapter 4

1 Manusov (2020)
2 Zinab Iskandarani, Head of Unit, Municipality of Lund, LinkedIn 2019–05–21
3 Helms and Haynes (1992)
4 Rogers and Roethlisberger (1952)
5 Covey (2022)

6 https://tompeters.com/2009/04/the-strategic-importance-of-listening/
7 Jones et al. (2016)
8 Kluger and Itzchakov (2022)
9 Brownell (2020)
10 Cooper (1997)
11 Brownell (2012)
12 Shotter (2008)
13 Abrahams and Groysberg (2021)
14 Sinek (2010)
15 Wood Brooks and John (2018)
16 Asplund (1970, p. 126)
17 Wood Brooks and John (2018)
18 Purdy and Borisoff (1997, p. 3)
19 Itzchakov and Kluger (2017)

Chapter 5

1 Elvnäs (2017)
2 Iacocca (1984, s. 54)
3 Elvnäs (2017)
4 Charan (2012)
5 Alvesson et al. (2017)
6 Itzchakov and Kluger (2017)
7 Bryant and Sharer (2021), Itzchakov and Kluger (2017)
8 Bryant and Sharer (2021, p. 65)
9 Macnamara (2016)
10 Söderfjäll (2018)
11 Andersson et al. (2021)
12 Zerfass and Sherzada (2015)
13 Hill (2019)
14 Hill (2019)
15 Söderfjäll (2018)
16 Purdy and Borisoff (1997)
17 Brown (2018)
18 Söderfjäll (2018), Bryant and Sharer (2021)
19 Elvnäs (2017)
20 Bryant and Sharer (2021)
21 Söderfjäll (2018)
22 Helms and Haynes (1992)
23 Branson (2015)
24 Edmondson (2019)
25 Jordan et al. (2020)
26 Drucker (1955)
27 Jonsdottir and Fridriksdottir (2020)
28 Carlzon and Dyberg (2021, p. 65)
29 Elvnäs (2017)
30 Macnamara and Gregory (2018)
31 Daimler (2016)
32 Eichenauer et al. (2022)
33 Dasborough and Scandura (2022)
34 Omilion-Hodges and Baker (2014)
35 Peters (2021, p. 63)
36 Itzchakov and Kluger (2017)
37 Grint (2005)

38　Bryant and Sharer (2021)
39　Purdy and Borisoff (1997)
40　Elvnäs (2017)
41　Söderfjäll (2018)
42　Elvnäs (2017)
43　Lindeblad (2021)
44　Carlzon and Dyberg (2021, p. 65)
45　Grant (2021, p. 62)
46　Brown (2018)
47　Kegan and Lahey (2009)
48　Brown (2020)
49　Elvnäs (2017)
50　Söderfjäll (2018)
51　Kuo et al. (2022)
52　Grint (2005)
53　Wood Brooks and John (2018)
54　Lloyd et al. (2015)
55　Kentell and Wöhlecke-Haglund (2021, p. 9)
56　Buckingham and Goodall (2019)
57　Peters (2021, p. 112)
58　Bryant and Sharer (2021)
59　Bryant and Sharer (2021)
60　Battilana and Casciaro (2021)
61　Peters (2021)
62　Battilana and Casciaro (2021)
63　Söderfjäll (2018), Elvnäs (2017)

Chapter 6

1　Weber (1947)
2　Maravelias (2003)
3　Johnson et al. (2009)
4　Vie (2010)
5　Collinson (2006)
6　Alvesson and Blom (2019)
7　Velten et al. (2017)
8　For an in-depth discussion of the concept of follower—see Blom and Lundgren (2019)
9　Smircich and Morgan (1982)
10　Carlzon (2001)
11　Velten et al. (2017)
12　Andersson et al. (2021)
13　Velten et al. (2017)
14　Heide and Simonsson (2011)
15　Heide et al. (2018)
16　Heide and Simonsson (2019)
17　Mazzei and Ravazzani (2014)
18　Omilion-Hodges and Baker (2014)
19　Andersson (2019)
20　Andersson et al. (2021)
21　Jackson and Parry (2011)
22　Tufvesson (2017), Söderfjäll and Svensson (2020)
23　Tengblad et al. (2007)
24　Reed et al. (2016)

25 Wæraas and Dahle (2020)
26 Tufvesson (2017)
27 Ewerman (2015)
28 Ewerman (2015)
29 Macnamara (2016b)
30 www.management-issues.com/opinion/6050/10-questions-to-ask-your-customers/
31 Malmberg (2017)
32 Malmberg (2017, p. 131)

Chapter 7

1 Macnamara (2016b)
2 Gregory (2011)
3 Xue et al. (2010)
4 Flynn and Faulk (2008)
5 Barker and Watson (2000)
6 cf Billing (2011) who argues that female leadership is influenced by male norms.
7 Ewerman (2015)
8 Lewis (2019), Macnamara (2016b)
9 Normann (1975, 1983, 2001)
10 Skålén (2018)
11 Ewerman (2015)
12 Macnamara (2016a), Ruck (2021)
13 Grönroos (2015)
14 Grönroos (2015)
15 Dahlman and Heide (2020), Heide et al. (2019)
16 Neill and Bowen (2021b)
17 Grönroos (2015)
18 Macnamara (2016b)
19 Macnamara (2016b)
20 Grönroos (2015)
21 Barlow (1997)
22 Kristensson et al. (2014)
23 Neill and Bowen (2021a), Bryant and Sharer (2021)
24 Simonsson (2002)
25 Johansson et al. (2011)
26 Tourish and Robson (2006)
27 Mitchell (2003)
28 Tourish and Robson (2006)
29 Macnamara (2016b)
30 Lewis (2019, p. 122)
31 Macnamara (2016b)
32 Macnamara (2016b)
33 Macnamara (2016b)
34 Warner (2018)
35 Svingstedt (2003), see also Svingstedt (2005)
36 Ewerman (2015)
37 Tax and Brown (1998)
38 Macnamara and Gregory (2018)
39 Macnamara (2016b)
40 Bitner (1992)
41 Macnamara (2016b)
42 Weick (1984)

References

Abrahams, R., & Groysberg, B. (2021). How to become a better listener. *Harvard Business Review Digital Articles*, 12, 1–9.

Agarwal, S. (2020, May 30). *The essence of listening*. https://medium.com/ihearyou/the-essence-of-listening-a6aa59073170.

Alvesson, M. (1995). *Cultural perspectives on organizations*. Cambridge University Press.

Alvesson, M. (2022). *The triumph of emptiness: Consumption, higher education, and work organization*. Oxford University Press.

Alvesson, M., & Blom, M. (2019). Beyond leadership and followership. *Organizational Dynamics*, 48(1), 28–37.

Alvesson, M., Blom, M., & Sveningsson, S. (2017). *Reflexive leadership: Organising in an imperfect world*. Sage.

Alvesson, M., & Spicer, A. (2017). *The stupidity paradox: The power and pitfalls of functional stupidity at work*. Profile Books.

Alvesson, M., & Sveningsson, S. (2016). *Changing organizational culture: Cultural change work in progress*. Routledge.

Amin, I. A.-R., Amin, M. M., & Aly, M. A.-S. (2011). *A correlation study between efl strategic listening and listening comprehension skills among secondary school students*. Faculty of Education, Benha University.

Andersson, R. (2019). Employee communication responsibility: Its antecedents and implications for strategic communication management. *International Journal of Strategic Communication*, 13(1), 60–75.

Andersson, R., Heide, M., & Simonsson, C. (2021). *Communicative coworkership*. Lund University, Department of Strategic communication.

Andersson, T., Crevani, L., Eriksson-Zetterquist, U., & Tengblad, S. (2021). *Chefskap, ledarskap och medarbetarskap*. Studentlitteratur.

Ås, B. (1990). *De fem härskarteknikerna*. Riksorganisationen för kvinnojourer i Sverige.

Asplund, J. (1970). *Om undran inför samhället*. Argos.

Bang, H. (1999). *Organisationskultur*. Studentlitteratur.

Barker, L., & Watson, K. W. (2000). *Listen up: How to improve relationships, reduce stress, and be more productive by using the power of listening*. St Martin Press.

Barlow, J. (1997). *Klagomålet är en gåva!: Kundvård som strategiskt verktyg*. Svenska förlaget.

Battilana, J., & Casciaro, T. (2021). Don't let power corrupt you. *Harvard Business Review*, 99(5), 94–101.

Bavelas, J. B., Coates, L., & Johnson, T. (2000). Listeners as co-narrators. *Journal of Personality and Social Psychology*, 79(6), 941–952.

Beard, D., & Bodie, G. D. (2014). Listening research in the communication discipline. In P. J. Gehrke & W. M. Keith (Eds.), *The unfinished conversation: 100 years of communication studie*. Routledge.

Bergeron, J., & Laroche, M. (2009). The effects of perceived salesperson listening effectiveness in the financial industry. *Journal of Financial Services Marketing*, *14*(1), 6–25.

Billing, Y. D. (2011). Are women in management victims of the phantom of the male norm? *Gender, Work & Organization*, *18*(3), 298–317.

Bitner, M. J. (1992). Servicescapes: The impact of physical surroundings on customers and employees. *Journal of Marketing*, *56*(2), 57–71.

Blom, M., & Lundgren, M. (2019). The (in)voluntary follower. *Leadership*, *16*(2), 163–179.

Boorstin, D. (1985). *The image: A guide to pseudo-events in America*. Atheneum. (Original work published 1963)

Bornemark, J. (2018). *Det omätbaras renässans: En uppgörelse med pedanternas världsherravälde*. Volante.

Bragg, S. (2007). "It's not about systems, it's about relationships": Building a listening culture in a primary school. In D. Thiessen & A. Cook-Sather (Eds.), *International handbook of student experience in elementary and secondary school* (pp. 659–680). Springer.

Brandebo, M. F. (2021). *Tillitsskapande ledarskap: Från teori till praktik*. Studentlitteratur.

Branson, R. (2015). *The virgin way: How to listen, learn, laugh and lead*. Virgin Books.

Bringselius, L. (2021). *Tillitsbaserat ledarskap: Från pinnräknande till samskapande*. Komlitt.

Brown, B. (2015). *Daring greatly: How the courage to be vulnerable transforms the way we live, love, parent, and lead*. Penguin Life.

Brown, B. (2018). *Dare to lead: Brave work. Tough conversations. Whole hearts*. Random House.

Brown, B. (2020). *The Gifts of Imperfection*. Vermilion.

Browne, J., & Nuttall, R. (2013). *Beyond corporate social responsibility: Integrated external engagement*. Retrieved November 9, 2021, from www.mckinsey.com/business-functions/strategy-and-corporate-finance/our-insights/beyond-corporate-social-responsibility-integrated-external-engagement

Brownell, J. (2012). The listening fast track. In A. Sturman, J. Corgel, & R. Verma (Eds.), *Cornell on hospitality: How to be successful in the hospitality industry* (pp. 37–51). John Wiley & Sons.

Brownell, J. (2020). Training and developement. In D. L. Worthington & G. D. Bodie (Eds.), *The handbook of listening* (pp. 303–314). John Wiley & Sons.

Bryant, A., & Sharer, K. (2021). Are you really listening? *Harvard Business Review*, *99*(2), 80–87.

Buber, M. (1994). *I and thou*. T&T Clark. (Original work published 1923)

Buber, M. (1998). *Knowledge of man: Selected essays*. Humanity Books.

Buckingham, M., & Goodall, A. (2019). The feedback fallacy. *Harvard Business Review*, *97*(2), 92–101.

Burleson, B. R. (2011). A constructivist approach to listening. *International Journal of Listening*, *25*(1–2), 27–46.

Burrell, G., & Morgan, G. (1979). *Sociological paradigms and organizational analysis*. Gower.

Canel, M. J., Barandiarán, X., & Murphy, A. (2022). What does learning by listening bring to citizen engagement? Lessons from a government program. *Public Relations Review*, *48*(1).

Cardon, P. W., Power, G., & Huang, Y. (2019). Leadership communication on internal digital platforms, emotional capital, and corporate performance: The case for leader-centric listening. *International Journal of Business Communication*. https://doi.org/10.1177/2329488419828808.

Carey, J. (2009). *Communication as culture: Essays on media and society*. Routledge.

Carlyle, T. (1904). *Sartor resartus: The life and opinions of herr Teufelsdröck*. Chapman and Hall.

Carlzon, J. (2001). *Moments of truth*. HarperBusiness.

Carlzon, J., & Dyberg, N. (2021). *Se människan! Min berättelse om framgång, besvärliga personer och konsten att lyssna*. Volante.

Carnegie, D. (1936). *How to win friends and influence people*. Simon and Schuster.

Carnegie, D. (2017). *Listen! The art of effective communication*. GD Media.

Castleberry, S. B., Shepherd, C. D., & Ridnour, R. (1999). Effective interpersonal listening in the personal selling environment: Conceptualization, measurement, and nomological validity. *Journal of Marketing Theory and Practice, 7*(1), 30–38.

Castro, D. R., Anseel, F., Kluger, A. N., Lloyd, K. J., & Turjeman-Levi, Y. (2018). Mere listening effect on creativity and the mediating role of psychological safety. *Psychology of Aesthetics, Creativity, and the Arts, 12*(4), 489–502.

Charan, R. (2012). The discipline of listening. *Harvard Business Review Digital Articles*, pp. 2–4.

Chiang, J. T.-J., Chen, X.-P., Liu, H., Akutsu, S., & Wang, Z. (2020). We have emotions but can't show them! Authoritarian leadership, emotion suppression climate, and team performance. *Human Relations, 74*(7), 1082–1111.

Christensen, E., & Christensen, L. T. (2022). The interpellated voice: The social discipline of member communication. *Management Communication Quarterly, 36*(3), 496–519.

Clarke, R. A., & Eddy, R. P. (2017). *Warnings: Finding cassandras to stop catastrophes* (1st edition). HarperCollins.

Clausewitz, C. V. (1997). *On war*. Wordsworth.

Cole, R. E. (2011). Who was really at fault for the Toyota recalls? *The Atlantic*. https://www.theatlantic.com/business/archive/2011/05/who-was-really-at-fault-for-the-toyota-recalls/238076/.

Coleman, J. (2022). Critical thinking is about asking better questions. *Harvard Business Review Digital Articles*, pp. 1–5.

Collinson, D. (2006). Rethinking followership: A post-structuralist analysis of follower identities. *The Leadership Quarterly, 17*, 179–189.

Cooper, L. A. (1997). Listening competency in the workplace: A model for training. *Business Communication Quarterly, 60*(4), 75–84.

Covey, S. (2022). *The 7 habits of highly effective people*. Mango Media.

Dahlman, S., & Heide, M. (2020). *Strategic internal communication*. Routledge.

Daimler, M. (2016). Listening is an overlooked leadership tool. *Harvard Business Review*, pp. 2–5.

Dasborough, M. T., & Scandura, T. (2022). Leading through the crisis: "Hands off" or "hands-on"? *Journal of Leadership & Organizational Studies, 29*(2), 219–223.

Deal, T. E., & Kennedy, A. A. (2020). *Corporate cultures: The rites and rituals of corporate life*. Basic Books. (Original work published 1982)

Deetz, S. A. (2000). The a priori of the communication community and the hope for solving real problems. In S. Corman & M. S. Poole (Eds.), *Perspectives on organizational communication: Finding the common ground* (pp. 105–112). Guilford.

Drucker, P. F. (1955). *The practice of management*. Heinemann.

Edmondson, A. C. (1999). Psychological safety and learning behavior in work teams. *Administrative Science Quarterly, 44*(2), 350–383.

Edmondson, A. C. (2003a). Managing the risk of learning: Psychological safety in work teams. In M. West (Ed.), *International handbook of organizational teamwork and cooperative working* (pp. 255–276). Blackwell.

Edmondson, A. C. (2003b). Speaking up in the operating room: How team leaders promote learning in interdisciplinary action teams. *Journal of Management Studies, 40*(6), 1419–1452.

Edmondson, A. C. (2019). *The fearless organization: Creating psychological safety in the workplace for learning, innovation, and growth*. Wiley.

Eichenauer, C. J., Ryan, A. M., & Alanis, J. M. (2022). Leadership during crisis: An examination of supervisory leadership behavior and gender during Covid-19. *Journal of Leadership & Organizational Studies, 29*(2), 190–207.

Elvnäs, S. (2017). *Effektfull: Detaljerade studier av ledarskap—så ökar du effekten av din tid*. Volante.

Ewerman, D. (2015). *Kundupplevelse: Varför vissa organisationer lyckas . . . Och andra inte*. Volante.

Flynn, J., & Faulk, L. (2008). Listening in the workplace. *Kentucky Journal of Communication*, 27(1), 15–31.

Gans, R., & Zhan, M. (2022). A story about speaking up: Mediation effects of narrative persuasion on organizational voice intentions. *International Journal of Business Communication*, 1–27.

Glauser, M. J. (1984). Upward information flow in organizations: Review and conceptual analysis. *Human Relations*, 37(8), 613–643.

Gordon, M. (2011). Listening as embracing the other: Martin buber's philosophy of dialogue. *Educational Theory*, 61(2).

Grant, A. (2021). *Think again: The power of knowing what you don't know*. WH Allen.

Gregory, B. (2011). American public diplomacy: Enduring characteristics, elusive transformation. *Hague Journal of Diplomacy*, 6(2), 351–372.

Grint, K. (2005). Problems, problems, problems: The social construction of 'leadership'. *Human Relations*, 58(11), 1467–1494.

Grönroos, C. (2015). *Service management and marketing: Managing the service profit logic*. John Wiley & Sons.

Heide, M., & Simonsson, C. (2011). Putting co-workers in the limelight: New challenges for communication professionals. *International Journal of Strategic Communication*, 5(4), 201–220.

Heide, M., & Simonsson, C. (2019). *Internal crisis communication: Crisis awareness, leadership and coworkership*. Routledge.

Heide, M., Simonsson, C., Nothhaft, H., Andersson, R., & von Platen, S. (2019). *The communicative organisation: Final report*. Sveriges Kommunikatörer.

Heide, M., Simonsson, C., von Platen, S., & Falkheimer, J. (2018). Expanding the scope of strategic communication: Towards a holistic understanding of organizational complexity. *International Journal of Strategic Communication*, 12(4), 452–468.

Helms, M. M., & Haynes, P. J. (1992). Are you really listening? The benefit of effective intra-organizational listening. *Journal of Managerial Psychology*, 7(6), 17–21.

Hill, L. A. (2019). *Becoming a manager: How new managers master the challenges of leadership*. Harvard Business School Press.

Hurley, A., & Walczak, M. M. (2020). Audiology. In D. L. Worthington & G. D. Bodie (Eds.), *The handbook of listening* (pp. 89–101). John Wiley & Sons.

Iacocca, L. A. (1984). *Iacocca: An autobiography*. Bantam Books.

Itani, O. S., Goad, E. A., & Jaramillo, F. (2019). Building customer relationships while achieving sales performance results: Is listening the holy grail of sales? *Journal of Business Research*, 102, 120–130.

Itzchakov, G., DeMarree, K. G., Kluger, A. N., & Turjeman-Levi, Y. (2018). The listener sets the tone: High-quality listening increases attitude clarity and behavior-intention consequences. *Personality & Social Psychology Bulletin*, 44(5), 762–778.

Itzchakov, G., & Kluger, A. N. (2017). The listening circle: A simple tool to enhance listening and reduce extremism among employees. *Organizational Dynamics*, 46(4), 220–226.

Jackson, B., & Parry, K. W. (2011). *A very short fairly interesting and reasonably cheap book about studying leadership*. Sage.

Jarzabkowski, P., Balogun, J., & Seidl, D. (2007). Strategizing: The challenges of a practice perspective. *Human Relations*, 60(1), 5–27.

Jarzabkowski, P., Kavas, M., & Krull, E. (2021). It's practice. But is it strategy? Reinvigorating strategy-as-practice by rethinking consequentiality. *Organization Theory*, 2(3).

Johansson, C., Miller, V. D., & Hamrin, S. (2011). *Kommunikativt ledarskap: Definition, teori och centrala beteenden)*. Mittuniversitetet, Fakulteten för naturvetenskap teknik och medier, CORE. Tillgänglig: http://urn.kb.se/resolve?urn=urn:nbn:se:miun:diva-29126; http://miun.diva-portal.org/smash/get/diva2:1038859/FULLTEXT01.

Johnson, G., Melin, L., & Whittington, R. (2003). Micro strategy and strategizing: Towards an activity-based view. *Journal of Management Studies, 40*(1), 3–22.

Johnson, P., Wood, G., Brewster, C., & Brookes, M. (2009). The rise of post-bureaucracy: Theorists' fancy or organizational praxis? *International Sociology, 24*(1), 37–61.

Jones, S. M., Bodie, G. D., & Hughes, S. D. (2016). The impact of mindfulness on empathy, active listening, and perceived provisions of emotional support. *Communication Research, 46*(6), 1–28.

Jonsdottir, I. J., & Fridriksdottir, K. (2020). Active listening: Is it the forgotten dimension in managerial communication? *International Journal of Listening, 34*(3), 178–188.

Jordan, J., Wade, M., & Teracino, E. (2020). Every leader needs to navigate these 7 tensions. *Harvard Business Review.* https://hbr.org/2020/02/every-leader-needs-to-navigate-these . . . wAR1p3NJSXOt_FREsIMz6eM4FAae19WFxoTX102dl-7rL3ASNpoQMMpZaG58.

Kahn, W. A. (1990). Psychological conditions of personal engagement and disengagement at work. *The Academy of Management Journal, 12*(1), 692–724.

Kahneman, D., & Tversky, A. (1979). Prospect theory: An analysis of decision under risk. *Econometrica, 47*(2), 263–291.

Kåver, A., & Nilsonne, Å. (2007). *Tillsammans: Om medkänsla och bekräftelse.* Natur & Kultur.

Kegan, R., & Lahey, L. L. (2009). *Immunity to change: How to overcome it and unlock the potential in yourself and your organization.* Harvard Business Review Press.

Kentell, C., & Wöhlecke-Haglund, C. (2021). *Feedback(r)evolutionen: Frigör urkraften i feedback.* Waterglobe Productions.

Kirtley Johnston, M., & Reed, K. (2017). Listening environment and the bottom line: How a positive environment can improve financial outcomes. *International Journal of Listening, 31*(2), 71–79.

Kish-Gephart, J. J., Detert, J. R., Treviño, L. K., & Edmondson, A. C. (2009). Silenced by fear: The nature, sources, and consequences of fear at work. *Research in Organizational Behavior, 29*, 163–193.

Kluger, A. N., & Itzchakov, G. (2022). The power of listening at work. *Annual Review of Organizational Psychology and Organizational Behavior, 9*(1), 121–146.

Kristensson, P., Gustafsson, A., & Witell, L. (2014). *Tjänsteinnovation.* Studentlitteratur.

Kriz, T. D., Kluger, A. N., & Lyddy, C. J. (2021). Feeling heard: Experiences of listening (or not) at work. *Frontiers in Psychology, 12*, 659087.

Kuo, C.-C., Chang, K., & Cheng, S. (2022). Can manager's listening behavior benefit employees? Power distance may have the answer. *International Journal of Listening*, 1–15.

Langlinais, L. A. H., Heath A., & Houghton, J. D. (2022). Trust me: Interpersonal communication dominance as a tool for influencing interpersonal trust between coworkers. *International Journal of Business Communication*, 1–23.

Levinson, W., Roter, D. L., Mullooly, J. P., Dull, V. T., & Frankel, R. M. (1997). Physician-patient communication: The relationship with malpractice claims among primary care physicians and surgeon. *JAMA: Journal of the American Medical Association, 19*(7), 553–559.

Lewis, L. (2019). *The power of strategic listening* Rowman Littlefield.

Lewis, L. K. (1999). Disseminating information and soliciting input during planned organizational change. Implementers' targets, sources, and channels for communicating. *Management Communication Quarterly, 13*, 43–75.

Lindeblad, B. N. (2021). *Jag kan ha fel: Och andra visdomar från mitt liv som buddhistmunk.* Bonnier Fakta.

Lipetz, L., Kluger, A. N., & Bodie, G. D. (2018). Listening is listening is listening: Employees' perception of listening as a holistic phenomenon. *International Journal of Listening, 34*(2), 71–96.

Lloyd, K. J., Boer, D., Keller, J. W., & Voelpel, S. (2015). Is my boss really listening to me? The impact of perceived supervisor listening on emotional exhaustion, turnover intention, and organizational citizenship behavior. *Journal of Business Ethics, 130*(3), 509–524.

Lloyd, K. J., Boer, D., Kluger, A. N., & Voelpel, S. C. (2015). Building trust and feeling well: Examining intraindividual and interpersonal outcomes and underlying mechanisms of listening. *International Journal of Listening*, 29, 12–29.

Macnamara, J. (2016a). Organizational listening: Addressing a major gap in public relations theory and practice. *Journal of Public Relations Research*, 28(3–4), 146–169.

Macnamara, J. (2016b). *Organizational listening: The missing essential in public communication*. Peter Lang.

Macnamara, J. (2022). *Organizational listening—emerging theory & practice*. University of Technology Sydney, Australia.

Macnamara, J., & Gregory, A. (2018). Expanding evaluation to progress strategic communication: Beyond message tracking to open listening. *International Journal of Strategic Communication*, 12(4), 469–486.

Malmberg, A. R. (2017). *Ta skit! Och gör det till guld*. Mondial.

Manusov, V. (2020). Interpersonal communication. In D. L. Worthington & G. D. Bodie (Eds.), *The handbook of listening* (pp. 103–119). John Wiley & Sons.

Manusov, V., Stofleth, D., Harvey, J. A., & Crowley, J. P. (2020). Conditions and consequences of listening well for interpersonal relationships: Modeling active-empathic listening, social-emotional skills, trait mindfulness, and relational quality. *International Journal of Listening*, 34(2), 110–126.

Maravelias, C. (2003). Post-bureaucracy—control through professional freedom. *Journal of Organizational Change Management*, 1(5), 547–566.

Mazzei, A., & Ravazzani, S. (2014). Internal crisis communication strategies to protect trust relationships: A study of italian companies. *International Journal of Business Communication*, 1–19.

Mintzberg, H. (1973). *The nature of managerial work*. Harper & Row.

Mintzberg, H., Raisinghani, D., & Théorêt, A. (1976). The structure of "unstructured" decision processes. *Administrative Science Quarterly*, 21(2), 246–275.

Mitchell, J. (2003). *Hug your customers: Love the results*. Penguin.

Morrison, E. W. (2014). Employee voice and silence. *Annual Review of Organizational Psychology and Organizational Behavior*, 1(1), 173–197.

Morrison, E. W., & Milliken, F. J. (2000). Organizational silence: A barrier to change and development in a pluralistic world. *Academy of Management Review*, 25(4), 706–725.

Mower, D. S. (2020). Philosophy. In D. L. Worthington & G. D. Bodie (Eds.), *The handbook of listening* (pp. 217–237). Wiley.

Murphy, K. (2021). *You're not listening*. Random House.

Neill, M. S., & Bowen, S. A. (2021a). Employee perceptions of ethical listening in U.S. Organizations. *Public Relations Review*, 47(5).

Neill, M. S., & Bowen, S. A. (2021b). Ethical listening to employees during a pandemic: New approaches, barriers and lessons. *Journal of Communication Management*, 25(3), 276–297.

Nichols, R. G., & Stevens, L. A. (1957). Listening to people. *Harvard Business Review*, 35(5), 85–92.

Norinder, J. (2019). *Värderingsbaserat ledarskap: Mening, tillit och transformation*. Naturoch Kultur.

Normann, R. (1975). *Skapande företagsledning*. Bonnier Alba.

Normann, R. (1983). *Service management: Ledning och strategi i tjänsteproduktion*. Liber.

Normann, R. (2001). *När kartan förändrar affärslandskapet*. Liber.

Omilion-Hodges, L. M., & Baker, C. R. (2014). Everyday talk and convincing conversations: Utilizing strategic internal communication. *Business Horizons*, 57, 435–445.

Patterson, D. B. (2019). *The art of communicating: Effective communication for influence people and create empathy*. Independently Published.

Pery, S., Doytch, G., & Kluger, A. N. (2020). Management and leadership. In D. L. Worthington & G. D. Bodie (Eds.), *The handbook of listening* (pp. 163–179). John Wiley & Sons.

Peters, T. (2021). *Excellence now: Extreme humanism*. Networlding Publishing.

Peters, T. J., & Waterman, R. H. (1982). *In search of excellence: Lessons from America's best-run companies*. Harper & Row.

Pettigrew, A., Thomas, H., & Whittington, R. (2006). Strategic management: The strengths and limitations of a field. In A. Pettigrew, H. Thomas & R. Whittington (Eds.), *Handbook of strategy and management* (pp. 3–30). Sage.

Potipiroon, W., & Ford, M. T. (2021). Does leader humor influence employee voice? The mediating role of psychological safety and the moderating role of team humor. *Journal of Leadership & Organizational Studies, 28*(4), 415–428.

Purdy, M. (1991). Listening and community: The role of listening in community formation. *Journal of the International Listening Association, 5*, 51–67.

Purdy, M., & Borisoff, D. (1997). *Listening in everyday life: A personal and professional approach*. University Press of America.

Qin, Y. S., & Men, L. R. (2022). Exploring the impact of internal communication on employee psychological well-being during the Covid-19 pandemic: The mediating role of employee organizational trust. *International Journal of Business Communication*, 1–23.

Ramsey, R. P., & Sohi, R. S. (1997). Listening to your customers: The impact of perceived salesperson listening behavior on relationship outcomes. *Journal of the Academy of Marketing Science, 25*, 127–137.

Rashid, I. (2021). *Feelability: How we lost touch with life—and how we get it back*. Forlaget Indtryk.

Reed, K., Goolsby, J. R., & Johnston, M. K. (2016). Listening in and out: Listening to customers and employees to strengthen an integrated market-oriented system. *Journal of Business Research, 69*(9), 3591–3599.

Renander, B. (2010). *Konsten att lyssna—enkelt och djupt*. Kreativitetsutveckling.

Resnick, B. (2019). *Intellectual humility: The importance of knowing you might be wrong*. www.vox.com/science-and-health/2019/1/4/17989224/intellectual-humility-explained-psychology-replication.

Robson, D. (2019). *The intelligence trap: Why smart people do studie things and how to make wiser decisions*. Hodder & Stoughton.

Rogers, C. R. (1961). *On becoming a person: A therapist's view of psychotherapy*. Houghton Mifflin.

Rogers, C. R., & Farson, R. E. (1957). *Active listening*. Industrial Relations Center of the University of Chicago.

Rogers, C. R., & Roethlisberger, F. J. (1952). Barriers and gateways to communication. *Harvard Business Review, 30*(4), 46–52.

Rönnberg, I. (2015). *Tala är silver—lyssna är guld*. Retrieved November 9, 2021, www. publikt.se/pa-jobbet/tala-ar-silver-lyssna-ar-guld-17658

Rosenberg, M. B. (2015). *Nonviolent communication: Ett språk för livet*. Friare liv.

Ruck, K. (2016). Informed employee voice. In K. Ruck (Ed.), *Exploring internal communication: Towards informed employee voice* (pp. 47–55). Routledge.

Ruck, K. (2021). Employee voice and internal listening: Towards dialogue in the workplace. In L. R. Men & A. Tkalac Verčič (Eds.), *Current trends and issues in internal communication. New perspectives in organizational communication*. Palgrave Macmillan. https://doi.org/10.1007/978-3-030-78213-9_6.

Ruck, K., Welch, M., & Menara, B. (2017). Employee voice: An antecedent to organisational engagement? *Public Relations Review, 43*(5), 904–914.

Rumelt, R. P. (2022). *The crux: How leaders become strategists*. Public Affairs.

Sahay, S. (2021). Organizational listening during organizational change: Perspectives of employees and executives. *International Journal of Listening*, 1–14.

Salisbury, J. R., & Chen, G.-M. (2007). An examination of the relationship between conversational sensitivity and listening styles. *Intercultural Communication Studies, XVI*(1).

Schramm, W. A. (1948). *Mass communications*. University of Illinois Press.

Schwartz, A. M. (1998). *Listening in a foreign language*. Center for International Education (ED).

Schwarz, G., Bouckenooghe, D., & Vakola, M. (2021). Organizational change failure: Framing the process of failing. *Human Relations*, 74(2), 159–179.

Schweidel, D. A., & Moe, W. W. (2014). Listening in on social media: A joint model of sentiment and venue format choice. *Journal of Marketing Research (JMR)*, 51(4), 387–402.

Senge, P. M. (1990). *The fifth discipline: The art & practice of the learning organization*. Currency Doubleday.

Shotter, J. (2008). Dialogism and polyphony in organizing theorizing in organization studies: Action guiding anticipations and the continuous creation of novelty. *Organization Studies*, 29(4), 501–524.

Simonsson, C. (2002). *Den kommunikativa utmaningen*. Lunds universitet.

Sinek, S. (2010). *How to listen*. https://sinekpartners.typepad.com/files/listen.pdf.

Sinek, S. (2011). *Start with why: How great leaders inspire everyone to take actions*. Penguin.

Skålén, P. (2018). *Service logic*. Studentlitteratur.

Smircich, L. (1983). Studying organizations as cultures. In G. Morgan (Ed.), *Beyond methods: Strategies for social research* (pp. 160–172). Sage.

Smircich, L., & Calás, M. B. (1987). Organizational culture: A critical assessment. In F. M. Jablin, L. L. Putnamn, K. H. Roberts & L. W. Porter (Eds.), *Handbook of organizational communication: An interdisciplinary perspective*. Sage.

Smircich, L., & Morgan, G. (1982). Leadership: The management of meaning. *The Journal of Applied Behavioral Science*, 18(3), 257–273.

Smircich, L., & Stubbart, C. (1985). Strategic management in an enacted world. *Academy of Management Review*, 10(4), 724–736.

Söderfjäll, S. (2018). *En liten bok om ledarskap*. Type and Tell.

Söderfjäll, S., & Svensson, C. (2020). *En liten bok om medarbetarskap*. Type & Tell.

Splitter, V., Jarzabkowski, P., & Seidl, D. (2021). Middle managers' struggle over their subject position in open strategy processes. *Journal of Management Studies*. https://doi.org/10.1111/joms.12776.

Statskontoret. (2015). *Att styra mot ökat förtroende—är det rätt väg?* (Om offentlig sektor). Statskontoret.

Stein, H. F. (2017). *Listening deeply: An approach to understand and consulting in organizational culture*. University of Missouri Press.

Svingstedt, A. (2003). Personalen viktigare än kunderna. *Dagens Handel*.

Svingstedt, A. (2005). Många servicemöten lämnar inga goda minnen efter sig: En praktikers reflektion. In H. Corvellec & H. Lindquist (Eds.), *Servicemötet: Multidiciplinära öppningar* (pp. 37–46). Liber.

Tax, S. S., & Brown, S. W. (1998). Recovering and learning from service failures. *Sloan Management Review*, 40(1), 75–88.

Telléus, A. (2020). *Konsten att lyssna: Vägen till större tillit och bättre relationer*. Strawberry förlag.

Tengblad, S., Hällstén, F., Ackerman, C., & Velten, J. (2007). *Medarbetarskap: Från ord till handling!* Liber.

Thorsell, K. (2016, Juni 21). Drömchefen är coachande och lyhörd. *KvalitetsMagasinet*. https://kvalitetsmagasinet.se/dromchefen-ar-coachande-och-lyhord/.

Tourish, D. (2005). Critical upward communication: Ten commandments for improving strategy and decision making. *Long Range Planning*, 38(5), 485–503.

Tourish, D., & Hargie, O. (2004). Motivating critical upward communication: A key challenge for management decision making. In D. Tourish & O. Hargie (Eds.), *Key issues in organizational communication* (pp. 188–204). Routledge.

Tourish, D., & Robson, P. (2006). Sensemaking and the distortion of critical upward communication in organizations. *Journal of Management Studies*, 43(4), 711–730.

Tufvesson, A. (2017). *Aktivt medarbetarskap*. Liber.

Velten, J., Tengblad, S., & Heggen, R. (2017). *Medarbetarskap—så får du dina medarbetare att ta initiativ och känna ansvar*. Liber.

Vie, O. E. (2010). Have post-bureaucratic changes occurred in managerial work? *European Management Journal*, 28(3), 182–194.

Wadström, P., Schriber, S., Teigland, R., & Kaulio, M. (2017). *Strategi: Arenan, affären, arbetssätten, ansvaret, avsikten*. Liber.

Wæraas, A., & Dahle, D. Y. (2020). When reputation management is people management: Implications for employee voice. *European Management Journal, 38*(2), 277–287.

Warner, P. (2018). *From surveys to transformation: Take your customer experience to the next level*. www.cmswire.com/customer-experience/from-surveys-to-transformation-take-your-customer-experience-to-the-next-level/.

Weber, M. (1947). *The theory of social and economic organization* (A. M. Henderson & T. Parsons, övers.). Free Press.

Weick, K. E. (1984). Small wins: Redefining the scale of social problems. *American Psychologist, 39*(1), 40–49.

Weick, K. E. (1995). *Sensemaking in organizations*. Sage.

Weick, K. E. (1998). Improvisation as a mindset for organizational analysis. *Organization Science: A Journal of the Institute of Management Sciences, 9*(5), 543–556.

Weick, K. E. (2002). Leadership when events don't play by the rules. *Reflections, 4*(1), 30–32.

Weick, K. E. (2020). Sensemaking, organizing, and surpassing: A handoff. *Journal of Management Studies, 57*(7), 1420–1431.

Wendelheim, A., & Rodell Lundgren, K. (2021). *Öppenhet och tillitsspiralen: Utveckling på riktigt*. Ekerlids förlag.

Whittington, R. (2001). *What is strategy and does it matter?* Thomson Learning.

Whittington, R. (2019). *Open strategy: Transparency and inclusion*. Oxford University Press.

Whittington, R., Regner, P., Regnér, P., Angwin, D., Johnson, G., & Scholes, K. (2020). *Exploring strategy*. Pearson.

Wood Brooks, A., & John, L. K. (2018). The surprising power of questions: It goes beyond exchanging information. *Harvard Business Review, 96*(3), 60–67.

Xue, Z., Majid, S., & Foo, S. (2010). Environmental scanning: An application of information literacy skills at the workplace. *Journal of Information Science, 36*(6), 719–732.

Yip, J., & Fisher, C. M. (2022). Listening in organizations: A synthesis and future agenda. *Academy of Management Annals, 16*(2), 657–679.

Yngve, V. (1970). *On getting a word in edgewise*. Chicago Linguistic Society.

Zerfass, A., Buhmann, A., Tench, R., Verčič, D., & Moreno, A. (2021). *European communication monitor 2021. Commtech and digital infrastructure, video-conferencing, and future roles for communication professionals. Results of a survey in 46 countries.* EUPRERA/EACD.

Zerfass, A., & Sherzada, M. (2015). Corporate communications from the CEO's perspective. *Corporate Communications: An International Journal, 20*(3), 291–309.

Zerfass, A., Verhoeven, P., Moreno, A., Tench, R., & Verčič, D. (2020). *European communication monitor 2020. Ethical challenges, gender issues, cyber security, and competence gaps in strategic communication. Results of a survey in 44 countries.* EUPRERA/EACD.

Zuboff, S. (2019). *The age of surveillance capitalism: The fight for the future at the new frontier of power*. Profile Books.

Index

Printed in the United States
by Baker & Taylor Publisher Services

Printed in the United States
by Baker & Taylor Publisher Services